still hungry in america

still hungry in america

text by Robert Coles · photographs by Al Clayton · introduction by Edward M. Kennedy

An **NAL** Book
THE WORLD PUBLISHING COMPANY
New York and Cleveland

In memory of

Robert Francis Kennedy

And to the millions of people like those in this book,
for whom he spoke and worked.

And they shall pass through it, hardly bestead and hungry;
and it shall come to pass, that when they shall be hungry,
they shall fret themselves and curse their king
and their God, and look upward.

And they shall look unto the earth; and behold
trouble and darkness, dimness of anguish;
and they shall be driven to darkness.

Isaiah 8:21-22

INTRODUCTION

On July 11th, 1967, I sat with my colleagues on the U.S. Senate Subcommittee on Employment, Manpower and Poverty and heard witnesses present hour after hour of disturbing testimony about hunger in America. When the day was over, many of us in the room could only feel shock and humiliation. I say humiliation because the hunger and malnutrition pinching the lives of thousands and thousands of American children can only be considered a moral disgrace — which lessens all of us as a people, and makes each of us as individual citizens feel shame and sorrow.

Perhaps more upsetting than anything else, than all the graphs and statistics, all the medical and nutritional facts put forward, were the photographs the witnesses showed: photo-graphs of men, women and children — white and black — whose faces showed unhappiness and pain, whose bodies demonstrated what chronic hunger does to the skin, the teeth, the arms and the legs of a human being. And we heard words too, words about what life is like for those same people and many others — who are tired and weak and desperate, but who, given a chance, are quite willing to speak their minds and let anyone interested know how unjust things can still be in this wealthy nation.

Senator Robert F. Kennedy heard that disturbing testimony also. And he saw the shocking conditions first-hand when he made a field trip with the Subcommittee to the Delta area of Mississippi. When this book's author, Dr. Robert Coles, appeared as a witness before the Subcommittee's hearings in Washington, Senator Kennedy made these comments in response to his testimony:

"I think the situation you have described has been intolerable, not only in the State of Mississippi, but I think for all of us as Americans.

"Something needs to be done. There is no question that we have the food, we have the wealth, we have the ability, as a number of you have said, to take care of these problems whether they are just in Mississippi, Alabama, New York, or wherever they might exist.

"Someone wrote a number of years ago that perhaps we cannot prevent this world from being a world in which children are tortured, but we can reduce the number of tortured children. If we don't do this, who else will do this? It seems to me it is our responsibility, all of us."

Now, through this book, those photographs and many more, and those words and many more, will reach a much larger audience than that present in the Senate hearing room. It was Mr. Clayton's sensitive camera that enabled us in the Senate to see what living can amount to when people work for the most meagre of wages (often they can find no work at all) and when they live in cabins, without proper sewage, or running water, or plumbing, and even — it turns out — without enough food. And from Dr. Coles, a physician and child psychiatrist who has worked with and studied poor people for many years, we heard how those same people feel, how they regard themselves and how they come to terms with their special fate.

I write this more than a year later, sure of one thing — that there are still children in this country who wake up hungry, who spend their days hungry, and who go to bed hungry. There are still children in this country who are born in broken-down cabins rather than in hospitals, and who grow up without ever seeing a physician or a dentist. Put differently, there are still children who feel pain and get no relief for it; who fall sick and get no medicines; who suffer accidents or injuries and learn to clench their fists and grit their teeth or cry long and hard — all to no avail. And there are still children, thousands of them, who simply do not know what orange juice is, who cannot take a piece of meat for granted, who look upon milk as a very special treat.

In other words, for thousands of American citizens, both white and black, young and old, survival itself can never be taken for granted. From meal to meal mothers worry what to do. Will there be enough? In fact, will there be anything? And from day to day children begin to learn their lessons: how to live with the dull, gnawing pain that goes with hunger; how to live with the weakness that goes with a diet low in calories; how to live with the vulnerability to disease that accompanies a diet low in proteins and vitamins and minerals — a general vulnerability or susceptibility which all too soon becomes concrete, in the form of stunted bodies, weakened and fractured bones and impaired minds.

It is not easy to talk about all this — and as a matter of fact, it is all too easy for most of us to put the whole unnerving problem aside. Isn't everything fine with us? Don't we have most of the good things of life? If we worry about food, it is because we have too much of it — and it is all good, tasty, attractive. We watch our weight — while others cannot have lunch and then for supper, day after day, take potatoes and bread and cola, and on good days some "meat" that is almost totally fat — all of which may not help keep poor people thin, but certainly shortens their lives. Our bones and muscles and skin and vital organs need certain vitamins and proteins, and without them promptly begin to wither and die. It is as simple and terrible as that.

In a sense then, I am very sad that this book has to be published. There is no reason why anyone in America has to go hungry. There is no reason why our fellow citizens have to live this way — the way they are shown and described living on these pages. There is no reason why mothers should have to talk to Dr. Coles the way they have, and there is no reason why Mr. Clayton should be able to find families like these all over — in the rural South and in Appalachia and also in our cities.

Yet I dare feel a measure of hope, because these dreadful conditions are being exposed, are being brought to our attention in the Congress, and are being documented in this powerful, compelling book, which spares the reader no truth but which treats its subjects — impoverished and defenseless people — with compassion and respect. Actually, for all their hurt and sorrow, the people we meet in this book emerge still alive and still struggling. They still have a flash and spark of spirit. We are asked to appreciate their stubborn effort to survive, to make do, to persist in spite of all the bad odds, all the hazards and obstacles that come their way. We are asked, that is, to know them as human beings, like us, whose dignity and worth if nothing else match our own. And we are asked to know, then act; and to act out of respect and admiration rather than because we are annoyed, or made a bit uncomfortable or ashamed. Could *we* survive such a life?

And so I cannot add much to this book; there is all too much in it already, too much suffering, too much tragedy. I can only say, yes, it is true; yes, it is real; yes, these are American citizens; yes, as a United States Senator I heard and witnessed more than a year ago what Dr. Coles and Mr. Clayton have heard and witnessed in so many states and counties; and finally yes, I share their sense of urgency, their sense of outrage, their determination that the world's richest and strongest nation will not forever turn a deaf ear and close its eyes to these, its own sons and daughters.

Washington, D.C.
August 19, 1968

The following photographs move from neighborhoods to people,
from children to parents to grandparents,
from rural areas to cities,
from the past—and still present—realities of farm life
to the new realities that factories and urban ghettos present.
The words do not necessarily go with the particular pictures,
but are meant to accompany them generally, and, sadly,
to spell out what it is like for people almost two hundred years after 1775,
and over one hundred years after 1865—
what it is like for people

still hungry in america

Before a child is born he has already lived a life; and when he is born he comes into more than the immediate world of his mother's arms. Not all pregnant women can take food and vitamins for granted, or a gynecologist to tell them they are indeed pregnant or an obstetrician to watch them and care for them and eventually deliver them a healthy son or daughter. For that matter, not all pregnant women can take for granted clean, running water, or a home that is warm in winter and reasonably free of germ-bearing flies and mosquitoes in summer. Nor can some pregnant women forget about rats and cockroaches, or garbage that is ignored by local "authorities," or sewage that is not adequately drained away. I am speaking here of *American* women, *American* mothers, *American* children.

These pictures are American pictures—just as I assume the sense of shame and sadness and compassion and honest indignation the pictures may set in motion are American emotions, naturally present in a nation founded in response to injustice and persecution. They happen to be pictures taken in rural Mississippi, in Appalachia, and in a great urban center, too — Atlanta, Georgia; and they happen to document the particularly awful fate of poor southern and poor Appalachian families. From my work in other sections of this country I can vouch for the more general significance of this stark, forceful, and unsparing collection of photographs.

2

I believe that it would be hard for the most partisan defender of the status quo to overlook the very specific nutritional and medical problems that afflict hundreds of thousands of American families — in 1968, when our Gross National Product edges toward the almost incomprehensible (and extraordinary and vastly influential) figure of a trillion dollars. It is important to all of us that not only medical eyes (though they, too, wherever they are) should witness the sights Mr. Clayton has recorded for this book. It is one thing for a doctor to listen to complaints, to record evidence of this or that; and it is one thing for him to write a report that summarizes his medical observations. It is quite another thing to capture the actual look and feel of privation — the expressions on faces that reveal the deep worries and hurts of people trying to make do as best they can, under harsh and harmful circumstances. Those writers — like James Agee and George Orwell — who have felt closest to the poor and tried hardest to tell what it is like to be desperately poor, have often given up in despair. They have not despaired

4

out of a particular professional inadequacy; they were good writers and knew how to put "situations" into words. They despaired because they were honest enough to know their own limitations as observers. So it is no accident that Agee's *Let Us Now Praise Famous Men* and Orwell's *The Road to Wigan Pier* both contain photographs. The lives of our southern tenant farmers or of British mine workers require honest, full comprehension; that is, any effort to convey what Agee calls the human *actuality* will have to be done by brothers working together — doctors and lawyers, writers and photographers, and in our time movie and television producers, with their wide-ranging capacity to evoke the scenery and circumstances of poverty.

A published photograph, in contrast to a documentary — whether written or filmed — makes a condition available for permanent inspection. A doctor's report, no matter how well written and clinically rich, still needs the reader's imagination. It is as if there are those sick, hungry, tired, demoralized people "down there" in the Delta and "up there" in the Appalachian mountains (or someplace else) and the doctor is pleading: "I saw them, and they have this or that wrong with them, and I was horrified, and I want you to know what I saw, what horrified me." Likewise, a film is a form of narrative. It is as if the sensitive television producer says: "Here is what is going on down there, and look at it, you viewers, in all its terrible continuity." On the other hand a picture, and particularly a series of them, is something else — perhaps a visual statement. One is asked

5

and more money, and more of — well, just about everything that most of us can assume to be present and thus forget about. In a sense, these pictures reveal how *need* can become a permanent condition, an ugly, dangerous, and hopeless condition.

These pictures also reveal what happens to the life-span of the poor, to the birthright of American children, to the growth — physical, psychological, spiritual — that *might* have occurred in millions of our fellow citizens. Hunger, pain — indeed, any medical complaint or symptom — cannot be neatly and conveniently separated from the world, in this case a world of dismal shacks, nonexistent or bad plumbing, and persisting garbage. Children not only grow physically and incur one or another disease; they also learn to live with what is *around* them. In my work with people very much like the people who appear in these photographs, I have to remember to let my eyes wander from the sores or scars, the lumps or swellings I see every day. Mountains of debris, contaminated water, faulty diets, poorly heated and overcrowded houses — all of that and more sets the stage for what in bacteriology I learned to call the "invasions" of bacteria, viruses, and parasites. Still, they live: the infants, children, youths, parents, grandparents and even great-grandparents who appear in this book. They live in spite of "invasions," in spite of hunger, in spite of illness, in spite of weariness, in spite of everything these pictures show — and more, too. Alive, these people might, could, would respond to anything better that might (but very well may not) come along. These pictures, then, offer us a mixed kind of spectacle, a terribly shameful, unsettling, and edifying view of the extreme distress and the redemptive possibilities that continue to exist, side by side, in the very same people — our people.

to stop, and take particular thought. Agee and Orwell knew that in the midst of their flowing descriptions of awful circumstances the reader had to have the static "reality," the visible coherence and impact that photographs offer. Writers can convey the "inner-world," and engage the sympathies of their readers; and doctors can indicate just how damaging the world can be to some of us. Yet it is the photographer who really confronts us — confronts us mercilessly with what others look like, and in what conditions they live, and how they present themselves to the world, nearby and (through the camera) far away, but not very far away.

If any Americans demand our *attention* — medical, nutritional, economic, political, and journalistic — it is the people one sees in these pictures. All physicians (whether they come from the outside to do research, or are longstanding residents of the several areas in which Mr. Clayton has worked) would have to agree, and in fact have agreed, that these citizens need assistance, need better food than they are getting, and better medical care, and better housing

6

Still, it is difficult for most of us to grasp the meaning of the lives Mr. Clayton has photographed. He has taken pictures, and now we "get the picture," awful and disheartening as it is. What is there to *say?* I sometimes wonder what indeed there is to say about the tenant farmers I know, or the children of the ghetto I am now getting to know. Sometimes, when I sit down to write up the life — the life history and often enough the case history — of one or another man or woman I've been talking with, the task seems hopeless. There is so much to communicate, and yet several of the snapshots my wife and I have taken seem to more than do it: everything, just about everything I would want to say seems *there,* in those Kodachromes, waiting for eyes that have any awareness and sympathy. And from a sharecropper's wife in Alabama I once heard my doubts more than confirmed:

> *People don't know what they don't see, I guess. There's no other way of explaining it, not that I can see. Out of sight, out of mind. You can't go telling them anything. No sir, I don't believe you can. They're used to shutting their eyes on you, but if you get them to stop and take a look around, then if they're the least bit partial to begin with, well they'll possibly come over to your side.*

8

YOU CAN'T FOOL GOD SO DON'T TRY TO BLUFF HIS SON

9

Actually what life was left in her had somehow sought out her eyes. They were like the eyes that stare out of the pages of this book. They were, that is, full of urgency, of demands. They appealed to one, but not because they were pretty or fetching — that kind of "appealing." Rather, they pleaded, and conveyed naked alarm. They were, after all, eyes that belonged to a woman who could also say this:

> From day to day I think to myself that
> God will stop it. I think He'll come down
> here and say something that will make
> it different hereabouts. He'll tell the
> people that they should stop doing like
> they do to one another, and they should
> hear His Word, and go do likewise. But
> until He comes, I'm afraid we're going to
> die all the time, way before it's time.
> I've lost three before they were even born.
> I've lost two before they were a year. I've
> lost two old enough — I thought — to live,
> to be full grown, the same as me and their
> father did. Yes, I've got me the six here
> who are still living, but let me tell you,
> I can never wake up in the morning
> without wondering whether we'll make it,
> one of us or all of us, until sundown.
> And that's the truth.

So, in one breath she can hope for the outsider's compassionate vision, and in the next she can pray for His Word, and go on to speak her own, to tell and tell and tell. And so I believe there are things to be told, things that can bring a series of pictures like these all that closer to her "truth." The reader should know how "those people" manage, what they feel, how they put together the separate scenes a photographer captures into the continuity of days, months, years. The reader should know what they say about and for themselves. Again from our sharecropper's wife: "They have deaf ears over in the county seat; but if only they would come near, I would see that they wouldn't turn their eyes away." So she spoke — and when I look at her photograph I can hear her words and recognize her need and right to be heard.

As a matter of fact, when I listen to her on one of my tapes I find myself in mild disagreement with her. Those men in the county seat, those "big men," know somewhere inside themselves that the truths to be conveyed by her plain, uneducated language are more than they could bear to hear. Yes, the sight of her cabin might make them blink and gawk, but they would quickly get out and move on. They have before. If only somehow they could be made to stay and listen — she hopes for that day, perhaps more vainly than she can bear to realize. By offering one picture after another, Mr. Clayton is suggesting we do more than glance, we look as she would like our eyes to look; and by describing what I have seen and heard in my work I am trying to do the same thing, to fasten our attention — before we once again take flight, take refuge in our comfortable important lives. To quote this woman once again:

> *Do you do anything with those records you get out of that machine? I don't mean to be disrespectful, no sir. I just mean, well my son James, he was asking if you went home and played us, like we was on the radio, you know. The same with the pictures. He said what do they do with them? Do a lot of other people see them, or do they keep hold of them to themselves? I said they goes to a college,*

maybe, and shows them around, and maybe they'll do something as a result, though to be honest I'm not sure what. I mean, people like you — I told my son that — they're not the ones who makes it bad for us anyway. So probably there isn't anything you can do to make it better. But James, well, he watches the cowboys and Indians, and he said no, that it wasn't so bad we couldn't win somehow — because a lot of times if the good people really stick to their guns, they win, but if they don't, then they lose, because they weren't paying attention, or they just lost their nerves or something. And the boss man, his nerves are always good, yes sir. He just watches and he never shakes or loses his voice, no sir — not like us.

11

To move from our "nerves," as sympathizers or well-wishers or bosses, to the nerves and muscles and bones of the people whom this book makes visible, we had best look at the first pictures, the ones *without* people, and consider, in an unpleasantly detailed way, what such an environment does to anyone, and particularly to children. Perhaps for a moment these pictures will persuade us to imagine what it means for a child to discover a rural shack or ghetto tenement and then assume the discovered to be natural or even ordained.

Nor am I speaking only of the so-called environment, the "outside" world. In the womb a child either gets the vitamins and proteins he needs or he doesn't. In the womb he either prospers and grows by incredible leaps or he responds to his mother's troubles, to the sickness she has and continues to have, to the hunger she feels and continues to feel, to the exhaustion that never leaves her. Picture not only what is shown here, but the days that follow one another for a pregnant woman. She sees the land being stripped and plundered for coal, but fortunately the child inside her is spared that. She sees a dreary shack and its littered, unsanitary "outsides," but again no "fetus," no newborn child has to know about all that. There comes a time, though, when each of us wants to eat, when we have to eat or die; and an infant without "knowing" it, needs certain kinds of food even more desperately than the rest of us, and so does an infant's mother. It is in the kitchen that an abstraction called the "environment" becomes *everything* for a child — whether unborn or born.

Any doctor knows this — but many people don't see any doctor. For the most part these people surely don't. If one of them is a mother and wonders whether she is pregnant she does not get her answer by taking a test. No one weighs her. No one asks whether there is any history of diabetes or hypertension or kidney disease in her family. No one takes pains to find out how her other children have managed if any were born — whether one or another congenital or hereditary disease has appeared in them. No one prescribes vitamin pills (with fluorides added) and no one recommends a particular diet, high in protein, low in fats and carbohydrates. And no one sits down with her and tells her that he, the doctor, will be *there* — to see her from month to month, then from week to week, and finally to wrest from her, amid pain and blood and, always, danger, a living breathing child, a new beginning who, as I've heard obstetricians say again and again, "may be President of the United States." Even the most tired and essentially fatuous clichés can express the force of human hope, of the aspiration that this set of possibilities will become — later on — a life of real and substantial achievement.

The womb protects not only the child but the mother, who does not have to see and hear what her own hunger or sadness or rage do to the infant for whom *she* is the "environment." We physicians now know — because we finally have taken the trouble to watch and watch — how quickly a newborn child accommodates himself to his mother, picks up her moods, responds to the quality and quantity of her care. We know that right off, in the first days of life, an infant senses and reacts as if things are going well, or picks up how badly it all goes — and yes, acts accordingly. All babies cry, but some scream endlessly and piercingly out of aching

hunger and because they are left to themselves — by mothers who cannot bear even to look at them or hold them for very long. An infant, after all, is a *reminder;* he or she is the occasion for a mother's realization, once again, that she, a woman, enables us all to persist, to see the future unfold in its most intimate and concrete form, childhood. Or an infant can prompt its mother to think of something else: it is all too much, too baffling, too frustrating, too awful even to contemplate — so away with him or her, whom I carried, whom I felt moving and kicking inside me, whom I now hear shrieking, see thrashing about, moving and kicking oh so restlessly out of a specific and unyielding hunger.

The rest of us, who have lived through the occasional, uncomfortable fears of our "colicky" infants have only to hear the pediatrician's words to feel reassured: it will pass; it is a stage; most children go through this; don't worry; we don't know what causes it; there isn't much of anything you can do; *it is not your fault.* Here, in contrast, is what any of the mothers in these pictures might have said, and repeated in the presence of, in memory of, each child:

I love to know I'm going to have one — when the period stops. I tell my husband I'm not coming around, and then after a while I know it's for real. You can feel everything in there growing, and it is good, yes it is. The time I worry is later, because it's a question of whether we can get into a hospital or not. Some don't try. They've been turned away, or they believe they will. But I've gone down there, and I tell them I live in the county, and please can't my child just be born there in the hospital, and I'll go home the same day,

15

or the next, if that's what they want. And twice they've been good to me and let me stay, and the other times I've had to go. It's up to the nurse; she runs the place. She has that doctor in her pocket. If she's in a good humor, she'll let you see him, and if not, well she tells you that hospitals take money to run, and why don't we quit begging. Now if you're real sick, I think maybe they're supposed to take you, and to deliver you also — they're supposed to.

But as I say, they either do or they don't, and you never know when you're walking up the stairs if you'll be walking back down again in five minutes, bleeding or not. One time I fainted and my husband, he had to drag me out, and he said the nurse, she told him I was faking, putting on some kind of act to scare her, and it wouldn't work. "You niggers sure must think we're dumb, falling for that. Go faint someplace else." That's what I heard later that she said. But there are good people, too — you know. Once my husband took me all the way to Birming-ham, and they were real nice there. They told me I'd been a bad girl, and I hadn't taken care of myself much at all. They told me I had swollen ankles, and why did I put all that salt on my food, and did I know it was hurting me, and my baby, too. They told me I wasn't eating right. They could tell even before they took their tests, and didn't I know that I was going to have a baby, and he needed to eat, and even if I didn't care much about myself, I

16

should think of him. Lord, they scolded me; but let me tell you, they were real good to me. They started in, and they took the blood, and had me give them some of my water to test, and they measured my blood pressure and listened to me all over. They said my heart was making funny noises, bad ones, but thank God the baby, he sounded all right in there, because they listened to him, too. And they sent me right on upstairs. They didn't ask me a single question, I mean whether I had a dollar to my name. They said I was sick, and I should get better, and that was all they cared about. And it was near time for me to deliver, so they did everything. I mean they got rid of the water and I lost weight. They said if I

18

didn't we'd both die, the baby and me,
especially the baby, so I was lucky to
come there. I near died, eating their
food, I'll admit. We're just not used to
having a lot of it, but with no salt. It
tasted funny, and a lot of the stuff — well,
I'd just never seen it before — them pieces
of meat with hardly no fat and milk all
the time and they'd give you puddings and
things like that, to build up your bones or
something, they said.

They say Birmingham is a mean town, a
real mean town. That's what I used to
hear as a girl; but I tell everyone it's not
so. I mean, it doesn't have to be. At
least it wasn't for me, that one time. Of
course the next time we came there, with
my girl Rachel in me, they were just like
around here. The man at the desk — he
wasn't no doctor or anything, I could tell
— he told me to turn myself around and
go right back where I came from. Then I
tried to explain to him what was the case,
and that I had a record there, but he
didn't want to listen. He told me that I'd
better watch my step. And he said they
didn't have room for any more people on
the "nigger ward," and if I got in last
time, well I was lucky. My husband was
getting ready to say something else when
the man reached for the phone — and
well, we both didn't say a word more. We
turned about real fast and walked out. All
the way home I thought they might be
following us, and we wouldn't hear the
end of it; but they never did, and we
were happy you know, after all that, to
have Mrs. Thomas come along and deliver

me, like before. I tried to stop with the
salt, like I remembered I should and
maybe that helped, because Rachel was
born a real good child, yelling and
screeching she did. But then she died, a
few months later. Yes sir, she did.

Why did Rachel die? I asked Rachel's mother, and she didn't know. I went to see Mrs. Thomas, a good midwife, not because she was trained but because she is intelligent and capable and has learned over the years (on her own) to deliver children adroitly, quickly, and confidently. She didn't know either, but she had no inclination to let my earnest, self-righteous, thoughtful, fair-minded inquiry go unchallenged. I went to her rather as a colleague, a woman who knows a lot about people who constantly protest how puzzled they are, how much they don't know. "I don't know" was Rachel's mother's reply, and I said to myself that maybe she doesn't, or maybe she does — but Mrs. Thomas, Mrs. Thomas will say more. *She* isn't so frightened, or slyly noncommittal. She has dealt with the white man. She is a leader. She is even an ally, an ally of the doctors whose concerns belong above, beyond, outside (take your choice) political or racial issues.

*I don't know. Don't you know? I mean,
you're the doctor. I have my ideas, and
once I tried to tell them to a doctor we
have around here, and what do you think
he had to say. Why, he told me that I
would be getting myself into a lot of
trouble, if I didn't watch myself and
stop coming out with ideas like that. He
said I'd best stay with the deliveries, and
not go following those children into their
old age, because if I did — well, that
wouldn't be like a midwife should, it
would be civil-rights work. And since to
be a midwife wasn't legal, except if he and
the sheriff said so — well, that's all.*

We continued. I prodded her. She became
in succession more polite and guarded, annoyed, forthright and rapidly thereafter, angry
at the likes of me, scornful of all my sincerity, my
unrelenting (medical, liberal) piety, and most of
all my cautious, judicious, scientific interest in
facts, in pinning down her "thoughts" and
gathering something called "evidence." The
more I tried to be considerate, or "understanding" or whatever, the more she seemed almost
appalled by me.

*I know you're looking to find out what's
going on, but we can't give you what you
want, because it's so bad here we don't
even pay much attention any more. It's
not that we don't care, it's just that
you know it happens all the time, and
there's nothing you can do, and nothing
anybody else wants to do. The mothers,
they say to me when I show them the
baby: "Mrs. Thomas, what do you think?*

*Will he live long? Mrs. Thomas, what do
you think? Will he make it?" You know
what they mean? You can't, I don't
believe you can. They're not asking me
anything. They're telling me something.
They're saying — they say it all the time
— that they keep on trying, keep on
bringing those babies into the world,
around here, and they have to — because
chances are most of them will die, be they
in good health at birth or not, they will.
That's what the mothers know, and that's
what even the children know, once they
get old enough to know anything. You
can hear them telling one another about
how this one died, and that one, and on
and on. That's one thing a little boy or
girl around here knows before he gets to
school, if he ever does get to school. He
knows he's alive. Do the children you
treat up there in the North, do they stop
and think they're alive? Down here that's
one of the luckiest things ever, to stay*

21

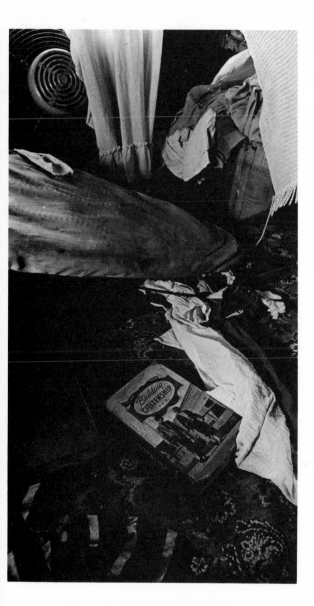

some have all they want and more, and we have nothing, a lot of nothing, more than we know what to do with, let me tell you. Well, my momma would tell me to stop, and to be grateful that I was alive to ask her all those questions.

Now Rachel, she died. She just died. There's no doctor hereabouts to save her, to look at her, to do something for her; so, how could there be one to find out what happened to her, and why she died. How could there be? But if you want my guess, I'll tell you, and then you can go figure out how wrong I am. To me it must have been a bad cold or something, and with a weak body, you know, well that's all it takes. I mean, she wasn't getting much food, and probably her mother's milk gave out, and when that happens — well, that's the protection God gives, even to us He does, and when that's gone, there's nothing left to take its place, nothing but luck. By luck I mean if you escape the germs, and if we don't have a harsh winter and freeze to death, and if God wrote down that this child, he just has to stay around, he has to or there won't be any one of them left. I doubt a lot of things about religion, these days I do, but I don't doubt what my grandma used to say — that some little babies, they're going to survive, come anything they're going to, because it's God's will that a few of us stay, and even the Klan, they can't scare Him. They claims Him, you know; but I don't believe He pays them much attention.

alive — yes it is. My mother used to tell me that when I complained and when I "bellyached," she called it (I was hungry, you know) and when I cried and when I asked her those questions, as kids do, the ones about why was it like this, and why do we have to take it, and why do

23

There was much more, a mixture I thought of shrewd, accurate observations and unconcealed cries of one sort or another. She was alone; the families she worked with never went to doctors, for reasons of childbirth or anything else. She was tired. She knew enough to feel cheated rather than fatalistic, angry rather than compliant. Yet, every day to survive she *had* to comply — and so my presence was doubly provocative. I stood for the oppressor, and yet I urged honesty and candor on her — very nice and helpful for me, but for her a terrible thing. The fact that my questions were medical ones made her even more uncomfortable and (I came to see) nervous and guilty — of all ironies, guilty:

> I wonder sometimes if I shouldn't be doing more. Yes, sir, I say to myself isn't there something I could do to save a few Rachels, just a few of them. I ask my husband, but he knows that it's me who knows, and we both know that the answer is no. But then I catch myself saying that maybe if I gave some of our food to them, and reminded them to boil the water all the time, and clean up as best they can,

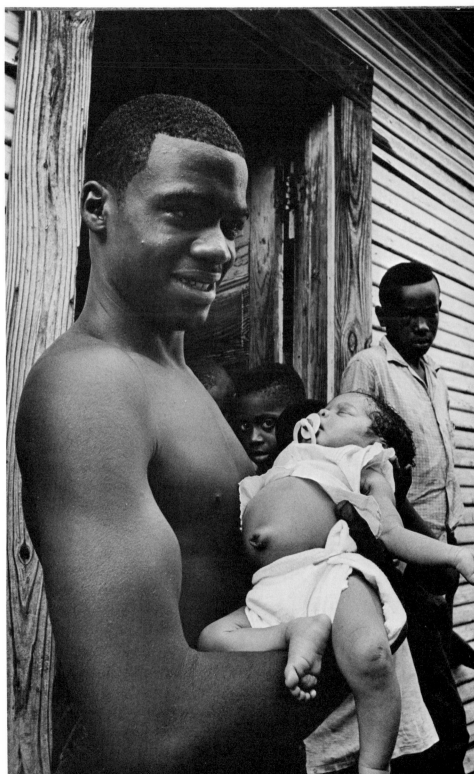

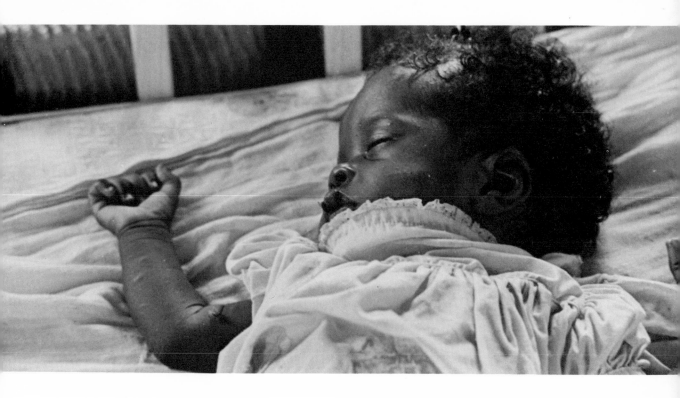

even with all the rest they have to do. Then I'll say that it's no good, trying to contradict things around here. Either the whole business changes and a girl like Rachel can live, or a person like me is wasting her time trying to do what she can't do. I'm here to deliver the kids, one after the other. If I stop doing that, and try to save them all the rest of their life — it just can't be done, not by a midwife like this here Mrs. Thomas.

As a clinical investigator, then, I have to conclude rather stiffly that we'll never know exactly what caused Rachel's death — what "took" Rachel. Eventually I did persuade Rachel's mother to describe the death, and as I looked and stared at these pictures, not only the ones showing children but the first few, I thought of what I once heard:

She was doing fine, real fine. I thought she was going to be fine, too. I did. There wasn't a thing wrong with her, and suddenly she was in real trouble, bad trouble, yes sir, she was. She started coughing, like her throat was hurting, and I thought she must be catching a cold or something. I thought I'd better go get

her some water, but it wasn't easy, because there were the other kids, and it's far away to go. So I sent my husband when he came home, and I tried to hold her, and I sang and sang, and it helped. But she got real hot, and she was sleepy all right, but I knew it wasn't good, no sir. I'd rather hear her cry, that's what I kept saying. My boy, he know it too. He said, "Ma, she's real quiet, isn't she?" Then I started praying, and I thought maybe it'll go the way it came, real fast, and by morning there won't be anything but Rachel feeling a little tired, that's all. We got the water to her, and I tried to get her to take something, a little cereal, like she was doing all along. I didn't have any more milk — maybe that's how it started. And I had a can of tomato juice, that we had in case of real trouble, and I opened it and tried to get it down her. But she'd throw it all back at me, and I gave up, to tell the truth. I figured it was best to let her rest, and then she could fight back with all the strength she had, and as I said, maybe by the morning she'd be the winner, and then I could go get a bottle of milk from my boss man and we could really care for her real good, until she'd be back to her self again. But it got worse, I guess, and by morning she was so bad there was nothing she'd take, and hot all over, she was hot all over. And then she went, all of a sudden. There was no more breathing, and it must have been around noon by the light.

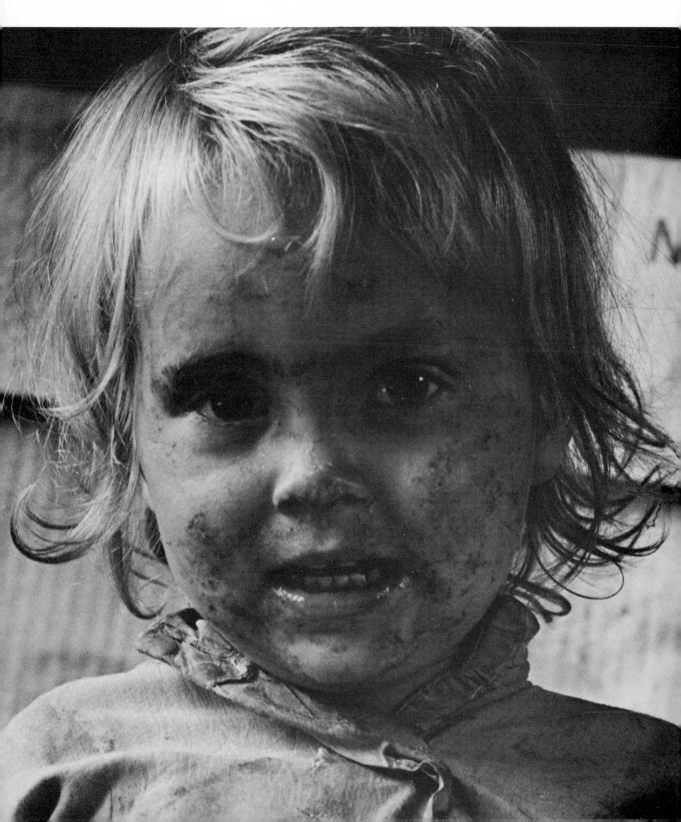

Doctors like me talk about the high "infant mortality rate" that continues to be recorded in counties where girls like Rachel are born, where the people Mr. Clayton has photographed live. (America, the world's richest, mightiest nation, has an infant mortality rate that is higher than that of ten other nations.) Why do these American children die so young? Why do other Americans live only to accumulate one disease after another? I suppose that we have to ask those questions and answer them very precisely, Mrs. Thomas and her common sense and her straightforward indignation notwithstanding. We want to know, know precisely and specifically. It is our "right" to know. Among other possessions we have that right.

All right then: from the moment of conception the hazards and burdens and risks and dangers begin to accumulate. A pregnant woman has special needs. She needs — the child inside her needs — vitamins and minerals. She needs protection against diseases like measles, which in its brief and apparently harmless course can hopelessly damage the growing fetus. She needs protection against other diseases, too, that occur in childbearing women and affect the heart, the kidneys, and of course the baby yet unborn. And she often needs rest, particularly in the first weeks, when spontaneous abortions occur, or in the last weeks when the entire body has to work harder to keep two people alive.

What does a woman like Rachel's mother get? Does a doctor see her and talk with her and watch over her during those fateful nine months? Does he examine her in the beginning and follow her along and then deliver her of child? "If we're real lucky we gets in about an hour before, and they'll help you, like Mrs. Thomas does — only you can tell your child he was born in the hospital, yes sir, like a lot of other children, I guess . . . but not many around here."

Nearly every day — like thousands of other doctors — I receive samples from drug companies. Recently one came that was specially designed for "nutritional supplementation." It had vitamin B_1 and vitamin B_2 and vitamin B_6 and vitamin B_{12}. It had niacin and calcium and folic acid. It had vitamin C. It is meant to help, among others, pregnant women. It is meant to help well-fed, well-clothed women during a period of special stress. It is meant for doctors — who prescribe what is "best" for their patients. A high-protein diet may be fine, but there is no point in taking chances, not when the issue is the welfare of the next generation.

Obviously the women shown here aren't going to get the Berocca tablets that Roche Laboratories sent me. Nor will they even hear a high-protein diet recommended, let alone receive one. If they start bleeding early in pregnancy they will go about their work. They will take care of the children they already have. They will go work in the bossman's house, and take care of his children, too. Or they might work in the fields. Even with mechanization, there is often need for field hands at the height of harvest time. Whatever it is they do, there is always water to be carried, clothes to be begged, bought — yes, and sometimes stolen:

The last time I worked for the missus almost up to birth-time. She says I cook better than anyone else and she said it was good for me to be coming over, because it took my mind away from worrying. Well, I didn't tell her no, because if I did, that would be the end of my job, and then I really would worry. Instead I stayed, and I had my lunch there all the week, and that's good, and I'll be honest and tell you that I got me a few things to wear — for the kids, not me. No, I'd never take anything for myself, but she has all those clothes, and just keeps them. Her kids are grown, all full-grown, but she keeps their clothes, two bureaus all packed. She never looks there, so I just took a couple of little suits. Yes, I did, and there they are, being worn. And I never told her, even when she paid me, when I almost did, but I didn't.

I gets my ten dollars from her every week, and that's all that keeps us from starving to death. And thank God there's my momma. She's pretty old, yes, but she takes care of my kids and she cooks for my husband while I'm cooking for the missus. He's not good, my husband, no sir. He's sick. He got hurt on his way to work. He was in a truck, with the others; they was driving the men to the fields. And suddenly there was an accident. Well, ever since then it's been even harder on us than before. They say he's all better, but I can't see how it can be true, because his leg hurts him and his back and his head — he gets dizzy spells. The doctor

32

come once after he got out of the hospital — they thought he might die — and he said we should forget about the accident and go back to normal. So he did, and tried to work. But the bossman, he come around and said we could all stay here in the cabin, but he didn't want any of us, not one, because he had the machines coming in. And why didn't we go North, that's what he asked. He said there isn't anything here any more for the colored man, and why don't we all go up North. I thought to myself then that he'd be sorry. I mean his wife would be, if we did, because there'd be no one like me cooking in their kitchen.

Her "missus" took her over to the county hospital to deliver a fourth child. An hour after they arrived there the little girl was born. The baby's mother had worked to the very end. Had no "missus" vouched for her, interceded for her, the cook might well have been refused at the hospital — which has a very small section for Negroes "who can afford to pay," as the "missus" herself put it when I talked with her. As for the cook, here is how she put it:

Down here they may tell you on paper that I can go anyplace and see a doctor, if it's something real bad, but even my missus, she'll admit that if a white man vouches for you, it's OK, and if you're a plain old nigger — well, it depends on what they want to do, the hospital people.

She has had convulsions in the past, as do thousands of pregnant women who suffer from eclampsia, from toxemia of pregnancy — a disease that strikes the rich as well as the poor. Yet much can be done to make eclampsia relatively harmless. Diets can be changed, salt restricted, if necessary a variety of drugs given. Women like this one, however, who cook for others and have to leave behind their own children, have no such medical luck. For them it is a matter — to use the words I hear again and again — of "prayer," of "waiting and hoping," of "seeing what will happen," of "relying on the next day when it will get better" or alternatively, of "preparing for tomorrow when the worst will come." In psychiatry we use the word "passive" to describe a certain psychological quality — to describe the kind of person who does not act, but is acted upon, who does not initiate things but rather waits for them to happen, who yields and submits and does the "taking" in the "give-and-take" of life. I fear that there are still other dimensions to human "passivity," medical and social dimensions that seem harder to deal with than the most intractable psychological symptoms.

When a child is successfully delivered he and his mother have survived a long, drawn-out crisis and a brief, dramatic one. Even under the best of circumstances women go through serious pain when they deliver a child; and there are a thousand complications or possible disasters to avoid. The child can become permanently injured by a prolonged delivery. He can emerge retarded, paralyzed, desperately sick. His mother can be seriously weakened. She may lose a lot of blood — and if she is anemic to begin with, that can be not only a serious but a fatal event. She may become infected, feverish, endangered by a "local" difficulty that has become a "systemic" one, that is spread all over the body.

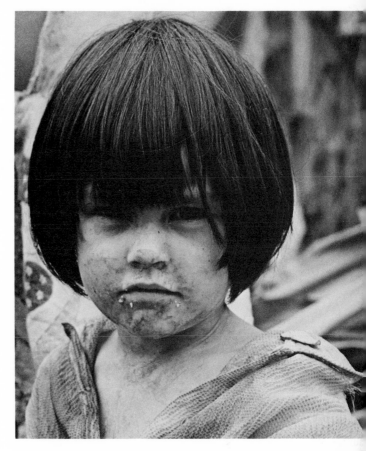

Or — miraculously it seems to the doctor, who knows all that can, that might, that often does go wrong — she and her children may do quite well, up in a hollow or in a sharecropper's cabin near the Mississippi River. They may not "come home," but be home; and in spite of all the medical care and attention they did not receive, they may surprise everyone (including their husbands and neighbors) by their "victory"

— that is the word I heard a mountain woman use. For those of us inclined to discredit much of today's knowledge or wealth as unnecessary and even immoral, weakening and corrupting, I can only offer portions of her remarks, easily used perhaps for "support" of such a "position" or "philosophy" or whatever:

You have your boy or your girl up here, and you feel like you've cut your way through the woods, sort of like we used to, I mean our forebears did. You're pretty much alone, and it's your doing. From what I hear on the radio, well they make so much of having their babies up there in the cities. Around here, you don't have your doctor to go see, and if you go to the hospital, that's only for a day or two, and you're out. A lot of us don't even do that, you know. There are the nurses who come help you, and me, I'd rather go through my pain here at home — anyway, it's so far, so real far to go to a hospital. Who can do it, and not end up having her baby on the road? When I feel the pains coming I tell my husband to stand by me, and we send for my sister, and she can always deliver me, and I can her — but she goes and tries to get a nurse from over the other side of the county, if she's able to come. But if she doesn't, I can manage alone. I got sick, bad sick twice, but I'm alive. And each time I feel like I've won a victory, all by myself, with no help, the way you do if you're fighting with someone, just the two of you.

The enemy? Oh, the enemy is the trouble you can get, the sickness, I guess. If you beat the sickness and you and your little baby are OK — after all the pains — then you've won your victory against getting sick, against being sick — and don't be sick if you can help it, my mother used to tell me. If I asked her how you can help it, she said we should pray every morning, and try to eat the best we can. But a lot of the time she didn't have all the food we wanted, and then she said we'd just have to hope we don't fall down sick, and pray we don't, and that's all we can do, pray, pray, pray.

What *do* they eat and drink — she and her husband and her children, and the others like them, black and white, all over the country? Some are lucky indeed; they can at least turn on a faucet and drink fresh water. Doctors know that water has no "food value," but that it is utterly necessary. The rest of us know that, too — the people in these pictures included. They may not have running water inside their homes, but some of them can walk to a nearby pipe and tap it. Some of them can't, though. They have to walk and walk — to a stream, a lake, a well, a spigot, and return home with their pails and buckets full. They have to rely on "nature" to keep what they bring home clear, a nature presumably unmolested by man. They have to summon what I can only call a kind of faith:

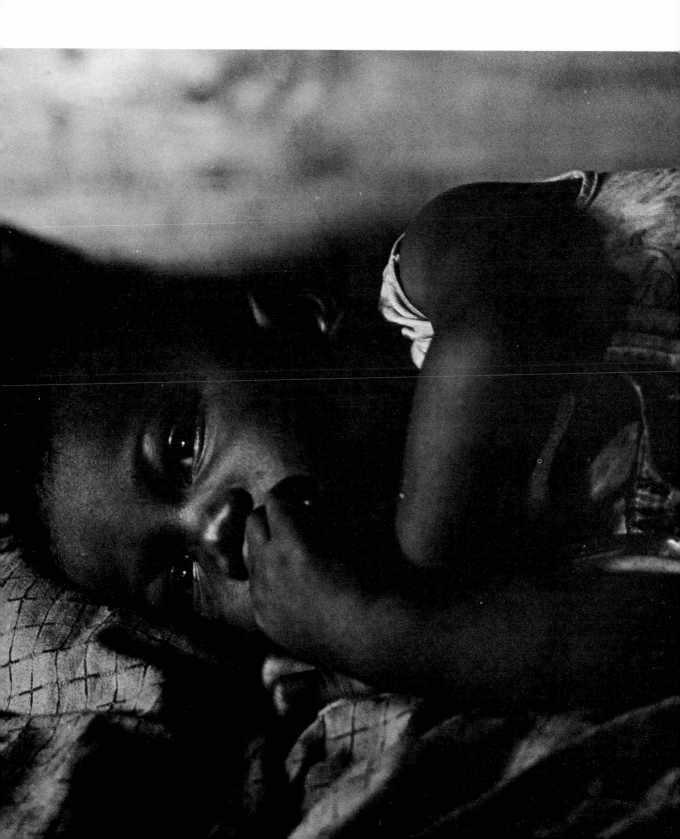

*It's pretty hard to know if the water's good
or if it's bad. There's a lot of it around,
but not for drinking. You have to get it
and hope it'll be good. Mostly it is, but
it isn't sometimes, too — I'll have to
admit. You know the strip-mining, it dirties
our water, more and more of it each year
that goes by. The more coal they dig, the
less water we can rely on. It's as simple as
that.*

And in the Delta of Mississippi, where no
coal is mined, the problem remains:

*There isn't no water here, no sir. We goes
down the road, yes sir. There's a faucet
he put in for us a while back, and it's the
best thing that happened to us, because
it saves you a few miles over to the store.
Yes sir, and they used to sell it to us in
bottles — to drink — that's right. And
of course we go and get it for ourselves, I
mean to wash up, that's from the stream
over there — oh, it's about two miles,
that's right.*

Somehow, then, they seek and find their
water to drink. Many never do trust the water
they get, and prefer Coca-Cola, Pepsi-Cola,
Seven-Up, Dr. Pepper — anything that is bot-
tled and "made for the rest of the people."
Besides, those drinks are also *food*, and food
that supplies quick energy. On matters like
water and carbonated beverages, I have often
found out how condescending my assumptions
can be. The people I'm observing — who re-
semble in every way the people in these photographs — live extremely hazardous lives, and

I assume that they know little and care less about the way the rest of us live, at least as far as "details" are concerned. They themselves have told me over and over again how little they know about "the outside," or about how difficult it is to get by, to make do. If life presses hard on them every minute, they can scarcely want to (or know how to) compare their fate with anyone else's. Yet they do, and more sharply than I once believed possible:

Here in Alabama if you're one of us, it's very bad, the water situation is. You spend a lot of your time worrying about water. That's the truth. You just don't begin a day without deciding who's going to get the water, and when, and how good it'll be when it comes back. That's why I use Coke for my children, right from the start I do. It's the best thing you can get to take away their thirst, and give them the sugar they need. They drink it all over the country; it's made for the rest of the people. If they use it, we can. We have to, though. We can't turn to much of anything else. There's the milk you have in your body to start out with, and that goes real fast — I hear say because we can't get enough for ourselves. My grandma, she used to say that nothing comes free, even a mother's milk; and that you plain run dry if you can't keep yourself fed up good. The one thing you can do is keep plenty of water inside, and that's what Cokes do, and as I say they give you your sugar. And when the babies get on their own they drink those Cokes and you can see them perk up, perk right up.

40

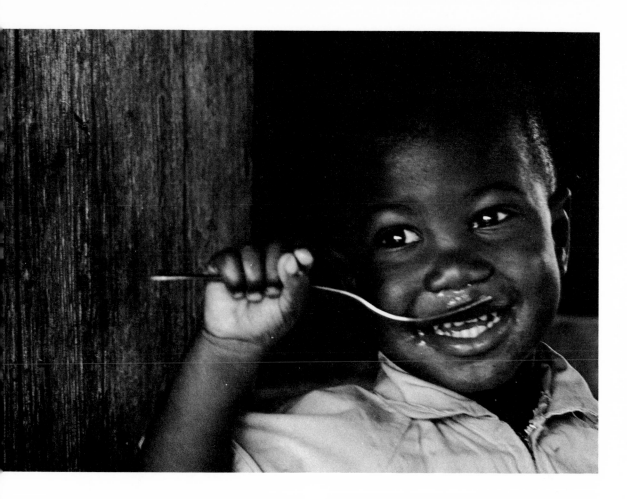

They'll be lying around, tired-like, and waiting on me to figure out what I can find for them, and then I'll get the bottle opener and they know what's coming. My grandma, she said we'd all be dried up and dead and gone from starvation if God didn't send us Cokes.

Didn't *they* cost money, too — those Cokes? Wouldn't a little milk be better than all that syrupy cola? How did it all get started, the habit, and what did poor farm people (or city people, too) do before carbonated drinks came along? Did a woman like that really believe that her well-to-do fellow citizens fed their infants and older children the same things she did? Had she any idea what endless cola drinks do to the teeth? Wasn't there some (unnecessary or "cultural") disposition at work, that

41

perhaps would yield to an educational program — given by nutritionists and physicians?
Those and other questions would cross my mind
as I talked with migrant farmers, sharecroppers,
and the mountain people of Kentucky or West
Virginia — and similar questions still occur to
me in the tenement flats I now visit, where once-
rural people now live — as they put it — "in the
city" or "up North." There is in my experience
no better way to comprehend the way millions
of poor Americans live than to get them talking
about *water* and *cola*. Their most devastating
problems come to light as they talk, problems
that have to do with poor sanitation, disease,
hunger, and perhaps most awful of all, the twin
senses of loneliness and lowliness. Here, from
my tapes, speak white men and black men,
white mothers and black mothers. Americans
all, they share a common fate:

> *Yes, a Coke costs. But everything costs
> and even if you don't have money, you
> have to pay. You get the money somehow,
> or mostly you just do work for somebody,
> and he pays for your Cokes and your
> flour, if you know what I mean. Me, I
> work in the house, and the boss man, he
> don't give me much money, but he helps
> us out, yes he does, with the food. He
> tells the grocer to give us some things, and
> he does, and he don't never bills us, no sir.*

*   *   *

> *Around here, you have to be careful. You
> go get water, and it turns out contami-
> nated. That's right. I tell my wife to give
> the kids water after she's boiled it, and
> in between to use a Coke or like that. A
> lot more people would be dead if we had
> to depend on river and spring water. The
> coal, the acid from strip-mining, it's getting
> into all our water.*

*   *   *

42

Yes, the nurse told me that milk is best, way better than a Coca-Cola. I said if she thought so, maybe she could come around here with a gallon or two, every day, and then I'd use it for sure. She said we should be smart, and sacrifice, and buy milk when we can, with the money we spend on Cokes. Then what do we do in between, I asked her. What do we do while we're saving up money to buy milk — tell our kids to be patient, and wait until we've got something for them to drink, maybe in another few days? Maybe those coal companies could give each one of us a gallon of milk every week; they'd still be making a fortune on what they take out of this here land. Even if I had the money to get a cow, and get milk from her, I couldn't let her around here to graze. She'd get poisoned by what they've done to our land; it's covered with slime, with the landslides those machines have caused. I hope the people who use our coal know that we don't get a cent out of it and can't afford milk, no, and our county, it's being torn into bits by what they do.

* * *

No, I don't think the Cokes hurt them. I think they feel better with a Coke. They have the bottle to hold, and it keeps them out of mischief, and they're glad to have something of their own, I'll tell you. My little boy, he got himself attached to an

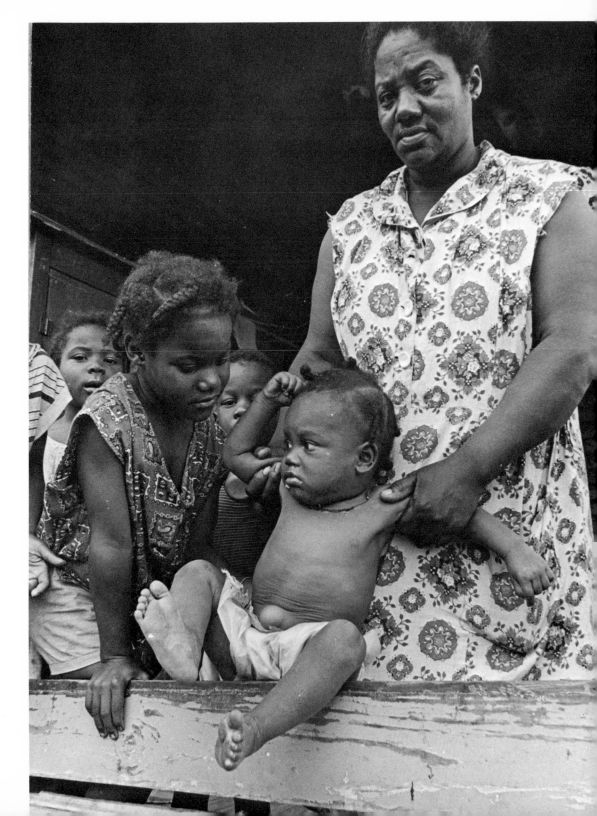

orange-pop bottle. It was the first time
he ever had orange-pop — no, he's never
had orange juice — and he liked it so
much that he kept asking me for more,
more, more. I said there wasn't any more,
not for now. Well, you know, he wasn't
really asking, I mean speaking. He was too
young. He just grabbed and grabbed, and
I thought, oh my, he really does like the
orange flavor, and we'll have to try to get
some more. My sister is up in Chicago,
you know. And she works in a factory
there, and she eats real oranges, and she
says she can keep a bowl of fruit around,
and why don't I come up there. But she
wrote it was bitter cold there, and besides
she don't be with her kids at all; it's my
aunt who's there and takes care of them,
so she can work, and they lives all in that
two rooms they've got, and nowhere for
the kids to go, or anywhere else. So it's
bad all over, that's what I believe. The
man at the store said that sure you might
get better food up there, but with the
sun and all down here, you don't need
so much. No, I don't believe he was
fooling me. He seemed to mean it;
though I admit I wondered myself how the
kids could get by on the sun and as much
food as he'd let me have from his store.
So, thank God for the commodities the
government gives us.

* * *

We'd be gone without government food, the commodities, you know, and we'd be gone without Cokes, too. I give my kids a Coke and they don't feel hungry no more. And I'm way along — I expect my baby next month, but even so I have to go get that water because we needs a lot and I try to help my husband, and he's tired after a day of cleaning up for the white man. He's one of the janitors in the motel down by the highway, and they pay him real good, twenty dollars by the week, and he can have his lunch. He's sure the fattest one in this family — only he can't get any of the white man's food over to us, that's the trouble. So, when he comes home the first thing we do is go get the water. Oh, it takes it out of you. One day if we ever get enough money, we'd like to move nearer to the town, where they has water inside. That would be something! But I'll tell you, thank God for the Cokes. If we get tired, we can always drink them, and the kids get quieted down real good on them — and they're pure, pure as it's possible to be, so you don't get sick on your stomach from bad water.

* * *

I hear tell that it's bad for our children, what they eat. The teacher, she said we don't do a good job of caring for them, and they shouldn't be having all those "soft drinks," she calls them, and they need more meat and eggs and milk and things like that. We're supposed to go buy them when they snap their fingers

and tell us to. And what do we use for money? Maybe they could tell the man at the store to give us back more money, on the bottles we bring in, and then we could buy the "protein" she keeps telling us about. Sure my kids have bad teeth. So did I and my mother and my daddy and as far back as it goes, probably. But what are we supposed to do? I see the missus and what she eats and her family eats. They don't worry how much this costs and how much that costs. I mean, they do: they talk about whether they can afford some land up there on a lake, for another home, to keep cool and go swimming in the summer. (They already has their air-conditioners, and those machines freeze me to death when I go there in the morning and I'm shaking all night when I get home, but it's good in between.) For us, though, it's different. I have to think every time I buy a loaf of bread. And I can't let my kids tell me they're hungry, they're hungry — because it drives me crazy hearing it, and I tell them to stop, and let me tell you, they know they've got to listen to me — or else. I say we're all hungry. That's the way it's got to be — and maybe one day you'll go out there and make a fortune. I don't know — I say that, too. I admit to them that it don't look like we will. I have to tell them the truth. That's how I talk to them; and they listen.

*   *   *

Here it's bad. These mountains haven't got a thing to offer but themselves. I like to live here, but it's getting worse and worse and worse. People don't have a cent, and there's no work, and we scrape by from day to day, and they're leaving, our young people, and they don't want to leave, no sir, but they have no choice about it. I think we're just about the least best off in America — the worst there is, I imagine. Other places they've got factories and money, and they have influence with the government, and all that. But here, no one cares a thing about us. We're lower than the niggers, I tell my friends that, and they smile and say "naturally." They don't even get sore, mind you. They're proud and they like to joke about things.

*   *   *

It can't be that it's any worse anyplace else. I'll tell you one thing, no white man lives like this. They all have their food and their water and their money. Even the ones that don't work — somehow they get taken care of. But not us.

*   *   *

Maybe we should become like the colored folks — start protesting, and all that. Maybe then we'd get our water pipes laid, and there'd be a job here for you, and a pile of that food — like they send it abroad to all those countries. Maybe then, but I don't think it'll ever happen. We're not made to protest here — though

we've tried and they put you down real fast, the sheriff and his boys. And there's no one out there beyond those hills to pay us much attention. They're all busy with themselves, and they've got a lot to keep themselves busy, so why should they bend over backward to help the next fellow. In the Bible we have, the family Bible — it goes back to 1823, and we were here before then, I know that — there's a letter from the first ancestor of mine to build a house and settle down. He said he was going to bless America every day for the rest of his life, and he was writing the letter to everyone who came after him, so that they would do the same, bless America every day of their lives, because of all it does for you. And when I was a boy that's what we had to do. My daddy said he wasn't so sure we should continue, but he said he didn't dare stop, or else we'd have nothing at all, not even what we can grow in the summer and use later — God would take everything. Well, He just about has, that's what I told the minister last year. He said no, it was a stage the country was going through, and things would get better someday. So, that's when I said OK, no more blessing America. We'll stay with church on Sunday, I said to my wife, but no more blessing of America, not until we can have at least one real good meal a week, and feel full for it — on Sunday, maybe; that would be a good day for it, Sunday.

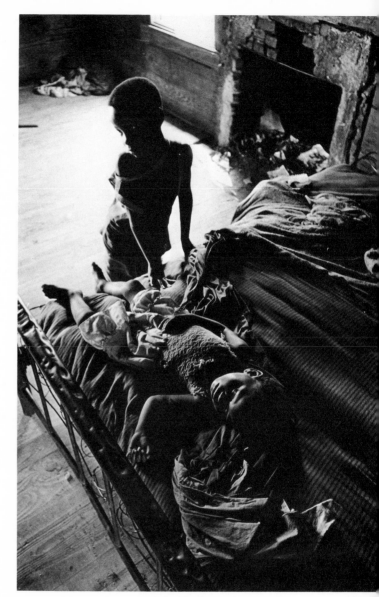

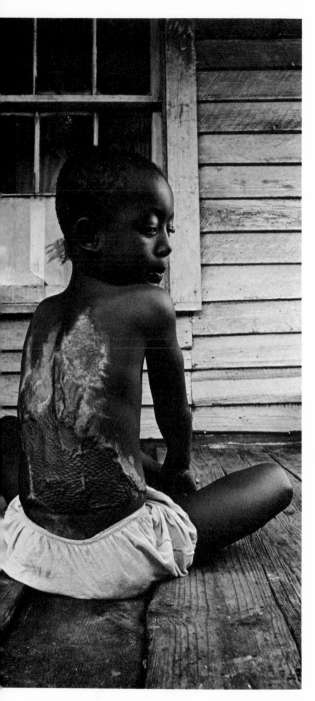

How do men and women like these — whose words you have just read, whose faces you can see here — actually spend their days, Sundays or otherwise? As Agee knew and pointed out so insistently in *Let Us Now Praise Famous Men,* no account of "life" as it is lived by any particular family (no matter how "representative" it is declared to be) can possibly do justice either to the people under description or certainly to others, who are preciously unique and different even in the way they face starvation and die — such is the ironic breadth of what a word like "individuality" can encompass. As I write these words I am surrounded by notes and tapes that come from many years' work with migrant farmers, southern tenant farmers or sharecroppers, and mountain families of Appalachia. Eventually I will have a number of *lives* "written up," but I hope not "explained" or turned into "types." Yet, we crave "lessons," and we want whatever generalizations the "trained observer" can offer. For some it is a matter of tidiness; for some it is an intolerance of ambiguity; for some there is "practicality" to insist upon, and the need for "answers," or those important things, "interpretations" or "recommendations." It is not enough that Mr. Clayton's photographs show us "the way it is" without a single word, or that in the course of my work I have recorded dozens of voices that plead openly and directly and quite simply for food, for shelters that actually offer shelter, for jobs, for an end to all sorts of obvious insults and humiliations.

Perhaps we need intricate theories because as a nation we have so far refused to do anything "about" or "for" such people; because we — the comfortable, well-educated, high-minded, sincere, and avowedly generous members of America's middle class — have said so often that something, anything *should* be done, only to find out how weak *we* are (politically) for all

55

the money and position we have; because the plain, blunt horror of what exists and what ought to be changed (and in America can be changed) makes our clever minds first ashamed, then challenged — yes, challenged to invent all sorts of face-saving camouflages, wordy and abstract formulations that make the awful and the dishonest seem by rights here to stay, out of some irremediable or terribly "complicated" or slow-changing "political reality" or "social phenomenon." And so social scientists or political scientists have got to be very careful; the legitimate inquiries they make as scholars can be used by any number of unscrupulous politicians and their followers to justify otherwise unconscionable delays, to support the formation of studies or commissions whose purposes are sometimes clear indeed: deflect what sentiment for *action* remains, appease what lingering outrage or shame persists, preserve "things" altogether, or give only the slightest ground, and in general postpone rather than encourage changes, no matter how urgently needed by millions of men, women, and children. It is one of the attributes of the human mind that it can brilliantly and convincingly shut out those millions of men, women, and children by discussing and analyzing them to death.

I say all this before going into a description of what is "done" from day to day by some poor people like those whom Mr. Clayton has photographed. I say all this because in West Virginia last summer a tall, blond, thin, brooding man whom I have known for three years let me know how he felt — apologetically, shyly, and then with unnerving force and anger:

57

We know you, my wife and I, and the kids, and we're not talking against you, you realize, not a bit. It's just that the other day I heard one of the VISTA people explode, at his own VISTA, and the more I heard him talk the better I liked it. He said he was sick and tired of all this pussy-footing around, and he said VISTA and things like that, they were just like putting on a Band-Aid when the patient is real bad sick, and needs a lot of surgery, yes sir. We got to talking, and I think it was his fault I exploded and said what I did, but when I came home and told it to my wife, what I said — well, she said I've been talking like that for years, and she was glad I finally told one of those "people," those "poverty workers," what I thought, what I truly thought.

It wasn't a long speech I gave him either. I just told him how a few years ago, like I told you before, they came over here, to this hollow and a lot of other ones. They said they were out of Charleston, and out of Washington, D.C., and they were going to get all the information together about us, and file a report, and then there'd be some laws passed or something, and we wouldn't have to live like this any more. So, they asked me and a lot of other guys what was the matter, and if we had our "choice" (can you figure that out — if we had our choice!) what would we want to do — in the line of work, I found out they meant. So I said: "Misters, I'm no loafer, and I don't want a goddam thing from you or anyone else. I'll do anything, so long as I can make enough money to feed my wife and kids. I can't bring myself to move out of here, I'll admit that. We've been here a couple hundred years, more or less, and we've given everything we have to the land here. When I was a miner I'd work all day until I could barely walk home, and if it wasn't for the union we'd have got nothing, nothing except enough to barely stay alive. For a few years they paid us pretty good, though considering you took your life in your hands every time you went down the mine, it wasn't all that much. Then they fired us all and took up strip-mining with the machines. It didn't make any difference to them, or to anyone else in the country, so far as I can see. In New England and New York or in the Rocky Mountains they were glad to get our coal, but when the companies got rid of us — that was just the way things happen. Then if we don't get new jobs, we're all supposed to move a thousand miles, over to Detroit or Cleveland and start life again. Is that fair?" I asked the men out of Washington doing their survey — I asked them that question and they looked as though they were annoyed because I was trying to change the subject and waste their time. I guess it's all right to treat us like waste, but you can't waste their time.

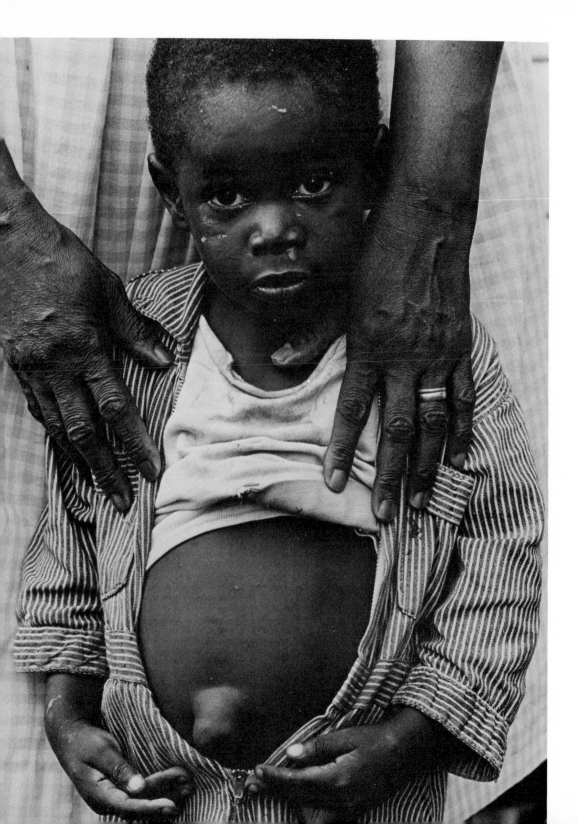

60

Anyway, I told the VISTA about it, about the long time I spent answering those questions. And do you know, that was way back. It was years ago. I don't remember how many, but near to ten, I'd say. Now the VISTA man, the young fellow, he means well. We all like him. But when he told me they were thinking of studying us again, and trying to figure out what they should do — that was it. For him, too, it was it. He said he just wanted me to know, and we might be asked to join and help out if some people came by wanting to look into things and ask questions — but he wanted me to know what he really thought. And that's how he got going, and me, after him. He told me about the new study, and I told him about the old one, and it lead to an afternoon we spent, exchanging our ideas.

I heard more, much of it only barely indirect, like the above quoted comments, and much of it — later on — right to the point of our conversation:

I hope you won't go telling people that we're a hopeless people right here. We've had a lot of people come through these parts and go off to let everyone know how bad it is, and how bad we are, and how it's no good. These mountains and us who live here we should move away, or start a big fight and march on the capitol, or be left alone, because that's the way we like it, and we don't like no one from outside — that's what the VISTA fellow told me he was taught. "Of course, I said to him." If you can tell me that, why then we're not getting along so bad, are we?" And he said, yes, that was right. But he and I agreed that there's a lot of bad talk about us from people who come here and then they go, pretty fast they're gone, and talking, talking about us "poor folks," and how it's awful sad about us, and aren't we the funniest people, the way we live, real peculiar they say, and isn't it the limit, us here all these years, and sticking to our guns, and keeping our habits like we do. The VISTA, he said there's books and books on that, to that effect, and what did I think. Well, he was joking with me, because he know for damned sure what I thought, and I told him I'd let you know, too.

So he did. Oh, he apologized after he did, and reminded me — as he did his friend from VISTA — that the fact we could speak so frankly was important, and meant we were friends, and proved wrong a lot of things said about mountain people. Yet he was worried, I was fairly certain, about what he had said. So it is with people who have grown accustomed to their own desperation, and to the callous, profitable, or elaborately rationalized indifference of others. To speak out is to take a risk. Why bother? But it is even a little risky and discomforting for people like *me* to speak out. That is why "responsible" observers have a tendency to take utterly overwhelming evidence and bury it in a thicket of "data" or comments that leave our institutions and leaders unthreatened, unbothered, even untouched — thus do we protect our own status. Indeed our attitudes toward poverty are reflected in the two distinct stereotypes we apply to it. In order to earn some cheap and quickly forgotten sympathy, the lives of perfectly respectable and determined people are caricatured and distorted so that they emerge as useless, semi-retarded, pitful creatures, in need of charity, a dole, a pittance. Or else those lives are made so exclusively "different," so intractable, so proud, so "happy," so uncomplicated, natural, unaffected, stoic, beautifully patient and enduring — that awe or envy becomes the only suitable and justifiable response from "us." But the people in this book are much more than the caricatures that middle class vanity or self-pity makes of them.

A sharecropper once told me about his "day," what he did from sunrise to sunset. Then he asked me whether I thought a lot of people were "living like that." I said yes, I thought a lot were; but also a lot weren't. His house for instance, is sturdier than a tent, and more comfortable than an igloo. On the other hand it is

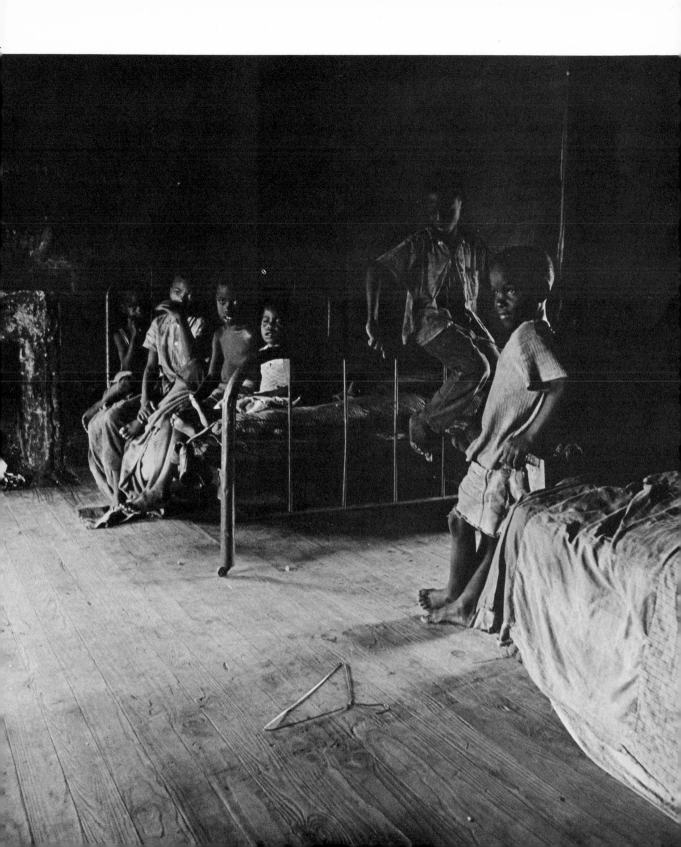

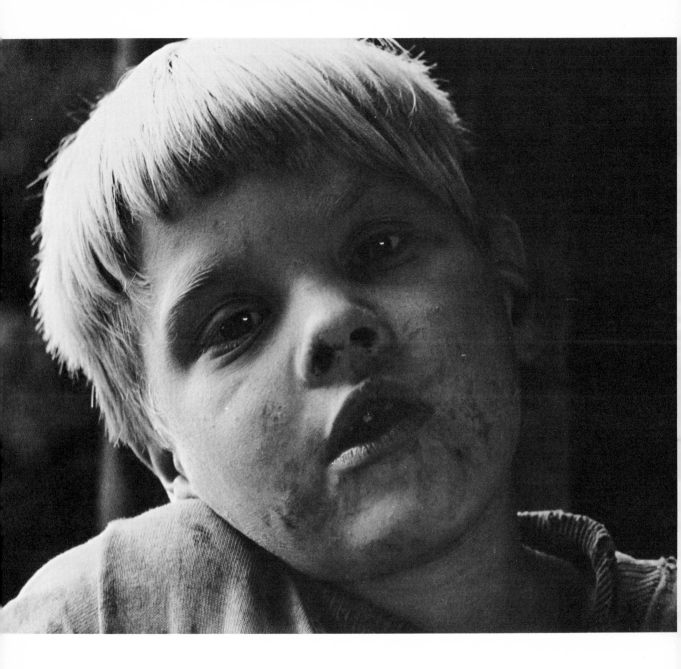

64

what a lot of us in America could only call a terrible shack, very much like the ones we find in this book. As one aproaches the building, the lack of sewerage pipes is obvious. In fact the cabin is unconnected to the rest of the world except for the wires that bring electricity to it — something, you will recall, that was accomplished in the thirties, now thirty years ago, when "rural electrification" was voted and implemented. Consequently, I know as I come near that I will find electric lights, and hopefully, but not always, a refrigerator. I can see the outhouse, so I know I won't find a bathroom, and I can see the pails near the door, so I know I won't find any source of running water. If I stay I will find out where to go for the water, where to fetch it, how to tote it or haul it — and I will learn that the day begins with the sun's light and the search for water: "One thing you have to say about here, there's always water, so long as you go to get it. It's no desert here, like I saw in the war." A veteran who fought for his country overseas, he now has one of the life-long advantages that travel can provide — a sense of perspective, an awareness that all privilege and all despair are relative.

And inside, what does one find inside? What stands past the walls, past the garbage that the town would not consider hauling off? People, of course, are what can be found inside those houses, even when the people are not immediately visible — if you are a stranger, dressed well and "looking into things." People are there, and the floors they walk on, the furniture they use, the ceilings that more or less provide cover for them. In my experience they are people who live exceptionally close together, sleep perhaps less than many of us, eat a good deal less than most of us, and stand a far better chance of dying young than the rest of us do. When they manage to stay alive into old age

they appear venerable, monumental, and in-credible — to their own kin, who likely as not at one time or other will say what this sixty-year-old man from eastern Kentucky did:

I'm sixty, and that's older by twenty years than I ever expected to live. I started feeling old when I was about thirty, and my friends would die — of tuberculosis, or killed in the mines, or there'd be pneumonia that would sweep through here like it was a rug my mother was shaking and beating, and we'd be the dust, just falling to the ground with each of the epidemics. They'd sometimes rush a doctor over here from somewhere, it got so bad, but he couldn't do much. We outnumbered him too much, the sick ones. When he took care of me, I asked him to tell me if I stood a good chance of dying and he said yes, truthfully, I did. So I said that was OK. My mother lost so many of my brothers and sisters, some before they was born and a lot after, too, that I felt lucky to be alive and a grown

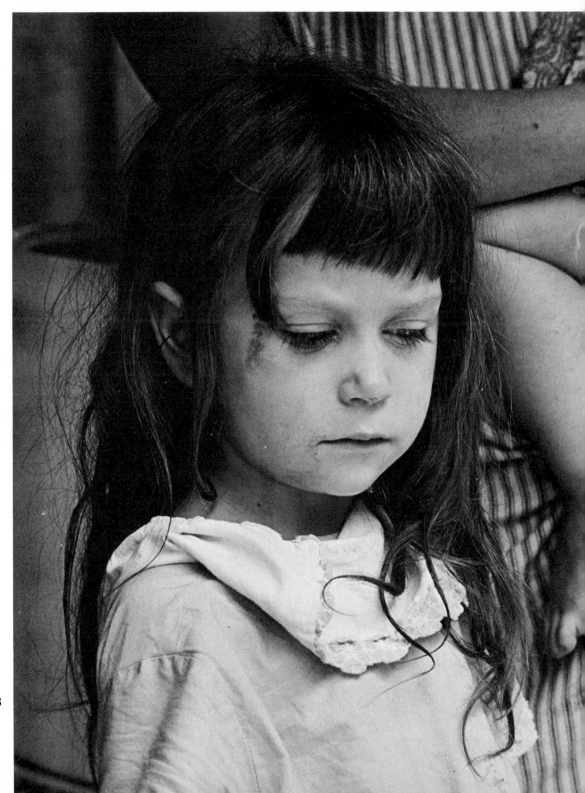

man. My father kept on saying that every year counts, because not many of us stick around long enough to get old — not like in other places, where they have a lot of people being sixty-five and seventy and on and on. But somehow I made it, through the pneumonia and another bout a couple of years later. I lost my teeth and my hair by the time I was forty, and I had a bad cough, and my lungs weren't good, and once I saw a doctor because I threw up fresh blood, and he told me I was lucky to be alive, but there was no point in my going over to Lexington or

someplace like that — the only thing to do was go home and pray that everything would be good. And somehow it was, you know. That's the "miracle," according to the doctor I last saw — three years ago. He said I was real "aged," but I was alive as I could be and that's better than being dead by a long shot. It's my wife's cooking I owe it to. She's the one who's really going to stay alive. I'm just lucky to have her. If she'd gone a long time ago, I know I would have followed her real fast, real fast.

They are close, he and his wife. They are also very close to their children and their grand-children. They don't recognize the privacy that we in the urban and suburban middle class cherish so dearly. They have a kitchen and they have two bedrooms. The kitchen is also a din-ing room and a living room. The bedrooms are that and no more. They have beds in them — no chairs and no bureaus. The kitchen also has beds, three of them. In that one house live fif-teen people: the grandparents and one of their daughters, already widowed at thirty-five, their son and his wife, the daughter's four children and the son's six children. They have a refrigera-tor, made in the forties, and an old-fashioned coal stove. They have an outhouse — so very cold in winter and in summer hard to use be-cause of the abiding stench, the inevitable and persistent flies and mosquitoes. They have heat, too: the stove and a gas burner placed at the other end of the kitchen, near the grandparents' bedroom. The kitchen also has a table, six chairs — three odd ones, and three that match — and an old sofa that has been patched and patched and patched. One window has curtains. The others have none. Each room has a socket and a bulb — 40 or 60 watts. There is no cellar to the house; it is on piles of bricks.

It hurts to call a flimsy wood-and-tar-paper shack a home but that is the truth of it — and in winter particularly the wind and cold make the floor seem more pretentious than anything else. For weeks they never take off their clothes and blankets are used by day as well as night. During all four seasons people sleep together. In winter they warm one another and in summer — well, they are there:

Yes I hear say you go to the city and if you can't find a job you can go on welfare — you can't here — and then you have to be careful, because they'll come around and tell you to give each child a bed, and things like that. If I had a million dollars I don't think I'd want to have my children scattered all over the house, not hearing each other breathe and living the loneliest life possible, it seems to me; to themselves, all to themselves. If I could have real good blankets, and if we could have another heater, and maybe a stove I could depend upon — then I'd be happier than with a lot more beds, yes sir.

I was asking her — the grandmother — what she might want, what *more* she wanted. I set no limits on her, but she was not about to take a blank check from me or anyone else. I suppose I should have noted how cautious she was, how "restricted" her "fantasies" were under my prodding. Instead, I was struck by how concrete and shrewd she was. The longer we talked that day, the longer I realized that for years she had been waiting for someone like me to invite her to dream, to ask her what she wanted and needed. She was a polite woman, and certainly not one to be demanding, to take wholesale advantage of a stranger's invitation — in order only to complain and criticize: "I keep the bad things that trouble us in mind, but I say to myself that maybe before I die most of them won't be here still troubling us. It might get better, you know." I might add that she and her family have no television and no automobile. Nor have any of them graduated from high school. Nor — so far as things go in their county — are they all that unusual in any of these respects.

In homes such as theirs or in similar homes I've come to know throughout the South the day begins at the latest with sunlight and often much before. Clocks are usually absent, and radios are not used to awaken families. When the mother or grandmother stirs and rises, all the rest get the message, move or thrash about and await expectantly her words, often a laconic "up" to the children or "ready" to the husband — which means coffee has been prepared, but not necessarily anything else, and often enough even that is missing. In other

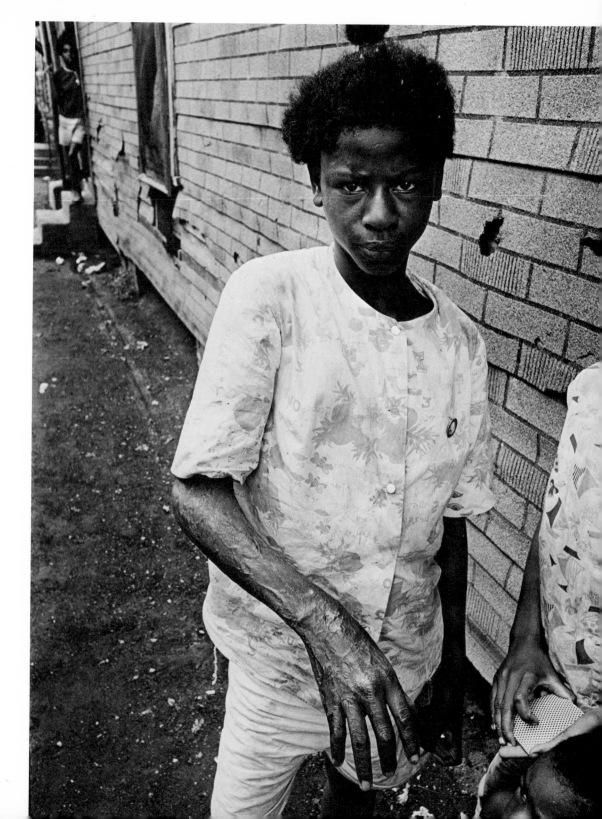

words, in thousands of American homes there is no such thing as breakfast. Mothers rise in order to get their children off to school, or their husbands off to the fields; or worse, mothers rise because that is what life is, days and nights — even for unemployed fathers and children without clothes enough to allow attendance at school.

It is awful and humiliating for me to mention such matters, to describe them, to ask you to comprehend the fact that this proud and terribly powerful nation (some fifty billion a year spent on guns and bombs — "military hardware" is the term one meets up with) has living in it by the thousands and thousands, white families and black families, whose men cannot bring in a penny of cash, week after week, and whose boys and girls have not the shoes and dresses and shirts and pants that enable them to attend school. So they stay home, and the laws that say they shouldn't are ignored not only by parents but by teachers and county officials who know all too clearly the restricted opportunities of education:

We don't get all the children in the county to school; we know that. I can tell you as superintendent that out there off the roads and especially near the fields a lot of them just don't have the desire to learn, and we're not set up to go seeking them out. I don't believe they're really suited for school — and our nigra teachers feel that even more strongly than I do. The principal of our nigra school calls them "primitives," and she wouldn't let them in even if they tried, which they don't. She wants every child dressed — wearing shoes if not

socks, and more than a tee-shirt and some worn-down dungarees or shorts full of holes. You know some of them, they walk around without any clothes all day, or maybe some underwear. In winter it's hard on them, real hard, so they can't very well come to school then, it's too cold to leave the house. A lot of them have Sunday clothes, though; they get dressed to go to church, if for nothing else. They're religious, even the most ignorant of them; no doubt about that.

To be honest, I just don't think they've got what it takes. I mean they're not endowed the way we are. But even if they are, it'll take a lot of doing to get them going — to make them feel it's of any use to go to school. I believe most of them think it's a waste of time; and they may be right. And I think they're afraid, too — of their own, I mean; they're afraid of the nigra teacher, even more than the nigra minister or the white man. Some of our nigra teachers are very strict. They have to be, I guess; and the people get scared. They think to themselves that they'll send their kid to school, and his clothes will be poor, and he won't behave the way he should, and he won't know how to use the fork and the spoon — yes, he'll want to eat with his hands — and the teacher will just blow her top and send him right home and tell him not to come back. That's what happens.

What happens is that children grow up to live apart — and feel apart. Minute by minute of each day they acquire their very own set of assumptions about the world. At night there is a bed for several of them, or indeed no bed at all. There are no books, and either nothing on the wall or a calendar, often with its reminder of the funeral director's address and telephone number, and its religious quote. In many southern or Appalachian homes I also see, I *still* see, a picture of John F. Kennedy. In his brief time as President he reached these people in a way that perhaps only Franklin D. Roosevelt did. And so I have to remind myself that if they are apart, they are also very much nearby, waiting and listening and dreaming and respoding in a flash to a man and a program that seem to be, at least, *theirs* — as well as everyone else's spokesman or property.

For the most part, though, the walls are barren, even without paper. So are the cupboards, where they exist. There may be some bottles of Coca-Cola, or Crown-cola ("R.C.") standing about on the floor or a table. There may be a loaf of bread, a jar of jam, a can of coffee, a carton of precious and carefully dispensed milk. And for the lucky, there may be a cardboard box with some "commodities" in it — government food, surplus food that a particular county has elected to receive and distribute to the hungry:

Yes sir — without the commodities I think all of us would be dead and gone. Once a month we go down to the courthouse and they gives them to us. There is flour, and dried beans. There is peanut butter and some meat, and they gives you dried milk, too. It doesn't last through the month, but it means we have something to eat, you know. And that's better than nothing. Some places, I hear the county people, the sheriff and his people, they won't let you have the commodities. And some places, they use the stamps. That means if you're on welfare you use the money you get to buy stamps. That means food costs less, because with stamps you can buy more; but you don't have money to spend on other things — clothes for the kids, and rent. So, I'll take the commodities to the food stamps, if you ask me. Because that's what happens when you don't have any money — and that's what it's like a lot of the time.

In dozens of counties (for example, in South Carolina the overwhelming majority of them) there is *no* provision of any kind for the hungry, the near-starving. One after another the county officials refuse to take advantage of existing federal programs, let alone press Washington, D.C., for more adequate ones. They refuse to receive commodities, things like flour and beans that have been declared "surplus" and are thus available to poor people declared by the local officials to be "eligible." They refuse to join the "food stamp program," under which, for example, a family of six whose income is one hundred and fifty-nine dollars a month can pay twenty-two dollars for stamps that will buy seventy-four dollars worth of food. They have even refused to take part in a federal program which provides loans to people whose incomes are so close to zero that they cannot muster a sum like twenty-two dollars a month for food stamps.

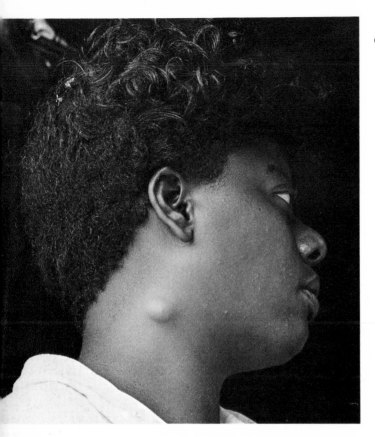

What, then, do thousands of hungry parents do?

I'll tell you, it's like this. I get up, and then I rouse up my husband, and then the kids move along. They pace themselves, going outside [to their outhouse] and then we does some talking, and if there's extra cornmeal, I'll fry it up. I have the baby to care for, and the other kids [there are five altogether] take care of themselves. We try to keep things in order, as best we can. I mean we sweeps up once a day. Then, most of the time the kids just play outside. I always try to send one to school. We have three old enough, but we only have clothes for the one. Mostly it's visits we have with my brothers, their wives and the children. They all play together, the kids. It's a lot of them — we could have our own school here, you see. And I makes something for everyone to eat — in the middle of the day. When the sun is strongest we come inside and it's cooler and we eat. And the kids will rest, and we have some fun. The kids go chasing after a fly, or they climb in and out of the windows. We might be having some people in, my brother or my husband's two sisters. And we'll sit and talk, and try to remember some of the funny things we can think of.

78

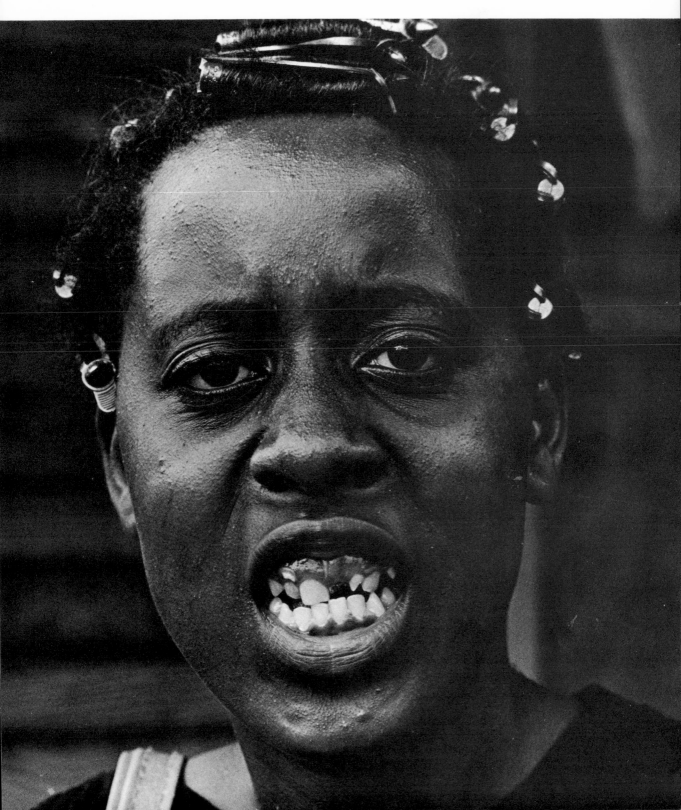

She manages to feed her children those midday meals — more fried cornmeal, some beans, on good days a piece of bread with peanut butter, and always the soft drink. In the afternoon everything begins to slow down. The children tend to be hungry (and so a bit slow) in the morning; in the afternoon they are "digesting the day's food" so that again "they slow down." By sundown they are all rather quiet; and usually they are asleep by seven or eight. Each one has a particular chore: to get water before it becomes dark or first thing in the morning, to put out the light by turning the bulb in the socket, to close the door — there is no bolt or lock — so that stray dogs or cats stay out.

The schoolteacher may talk of their "primitive" quality, but I find in their daily lives a definite rhythm, an almost desperate effort to find order, to achieve for each person at least a fragment of continuity, regularity, predictability, coherence — all that "we" strive for, too. Then, there is the Bible, and God's presence, talked about and deeply felt by these "backward" and "primitive" and "illiterate" and voteless people:

I teach my kids to wake up with a prayer and go to sleep with one. I hear them saying them, too; so I know I get them to believe. I tell them it's not the best here, but we may have another chance the next time around, and He's watching us, so we better be good. Sometimes my kids, when they're real young, they'll want to know if the white man is Him, God. I tell them no, he isn't. They think that because the white man is watching us all the time that I mean him when I talk of God

81

looking down on us; but they soon know the difference — between God and the white man, yes sir. And they learn to pray hard, real hard; and if they forget I remind them.

From time to time her husband works in the field. He does not pick cotton as he used to do — machines now have replaced him. He helps with a side-crop of corn and tomatoes. He does errands for a man who manages a large plantation. He rakes and "cleans up" around the house, "mostly outside." He also grows some flowers outside his own cabin, and he has some corn and tomatoes there, too. He hauls water, cuts wood, and from time to time goes into town — to pick up his commodities, to check in with a friend who is a delivery "boy" for a grocery market. If he would only desert his wife and children they might (but only might) collect a welfare check from the county:

It wouldn't be much — I think around fifty or seventy-five dollars, I don't know exactly — but it would be as much or more as I ever make on my own, and it would come in real regular, every month. Like it is, I'll make twenty or thirty dollars one week, and the next I don't hardly make anything. The bossman, he'll give me commodities, and that's good. But you can't expect him to support me — no sir, not now that he's got his machines. He said we could stay in the cabins all we want, that he wasn't going to plow us out and force us to go North, like some of the other bossmans do. But he couldn't do any more, he said, and didn't we agree. So I said, "Yes sir," and he said, "That's right." And I told him we'd try to stay,

because we hear it's not so good up there in Chicago, either, nor the other cities. I do hear you get more food, and you can go to a doctor for nothing and he'll see you, but they say you can get lost up there, and freeze to death, and they have big rats that jump on you. Me — I'm forty-five, too old to want to move, I guess. And I'm scared — to be honest with you — yes, scared.

If he and his family and others who live near them did go North they would present any medical clinic they visited with a shocking variety of what doctors sometimes summarize as "pathology." Let me describe what I have seen among fifty or so people who live in four small cabins at the edge of a large plantation. In child after child I have seen evidence of vitamin and mineral deficiencies; serious, untreated skin infections and ulcerations; eye and ear diseases; unattended bone diseases secondary to poor food intake; the prevalence of bacterial and parasitic disease, as well as severe anemia, with resulting loss of energy and ability to live a normally active life; diseases of the heart and the lungs — requiring surgery — which have gone undiagnosed and untreated; epileptic and other neurological disorders; a severe kidney ailment that in other children would warrant immediate hospitalization; and finally, evidence of what can properly and conservatively be called malnutrition, with consequent injury to the body's tissues — its muscles, bone, and skin — accompanied by a psychological state of malaise. Diarrhea, chronic sores, chronic leg and arm (untreated) injuries and deformities — they are everywhere around for a doctor to notice, and in time to overlook and forget.

83

I have to *remind* myself after a while that I am staying in homes that lack screens and running water and even on occasion electricity. I have to remind myself that mosquitoes and flies bear germs, as does stagnant water, that a meal of grits, bread, Kool-Aid or Coke, and occasional slices of "salad meat" or fatback gives the body some calories to burn, but precious little else. I have to remind myself, as a physician, that not all American children are plagued by illnesses with names like trichinosis, enterobiasis, ascariasis, or even a plain-worded one like hookworm disease. I have to keep in mind that dry skin, shrunken skin, ulcerated skin is rarely seen by the pediatricians who work with my children, with "our" children; nor are rashes, boils, abscesses, furuncles, impetigo, and scars the *usual* and *constant* thing to be found in child after child.

All that and more goes on. With five other doctors in May of 1967 I went from home to home in several counties of Mississippi. We were shocked, just as I had been horrified and ashamed all these past years. We wrote a report called "Children in Mississippi," and in July of 1967 presented our findings to a group of United States Senators — they were members of a subcommittee on employment, manpower, and poverty, and they listened to us and questioned us in a public hearing. (Some of these photographs were offered in evidence.) To quote myself:

Almost every child we saw was in a state of negative nitrogen balance; that is, a marked inadequacy of diet has led the body to consume its own protein tissue. What we saw clinically — the result of this condition of chronic hunger and malnutrition — was as follows: wasting of muscles; enlarged hearts; edematous legs and in some cases the presence of abdominal edema (so-called swollen or or bloated belly); spontaneous bleeding of the mouth or nose or evidence of internal hemorrhage; osteoporosis — a weakening of bone structure — and, as a consequence, fractures unrelated to injury or accident; and again and again, fatigue, exhaustion, weakness.

These children would need blood transfusions before any corrective surgery could be done — and we found in child after child (and in adults, too) the need for surgery: hernias; poorly healed fractures; rheumatic and congenital heart disease with attendant murmurs, difficult breathing, and chest pain; evidence of gastrointestinal bleeding or partial obstruction; severe, suppurating ear infections; congenital or developmental eye disease in bad need of correction.

The teeth of practically every child we saw — and of their parents, too — were in awful repair — eaten up by cavities and often poorly developed. Their gums showed how severely anemic these children are; and the gums were also infected and foul-smelling.

Many of these children (and again their parents) were suffering from degenerative joint diseases. Injuries had not been treated when they occurred. Bleeding had taken place, with subsequent infections. Now, at seven or eight, a child's knee joint or elbow joints might show the "range of action" that one finds in a man of seventy who suffers from crippling arthritis.

In child after child we tested for peripheral neuritis — and found it, secondary to untreated injuries, infections, and food deficiencies. These children could not feel normally — feel pressure or heat or cold or applied pain the way the normal person does. What they do feel is the sensory pain that goes with disease; pricking, burning, flashes of sharp pain, or a "deep pain" as one child put it.

The children were plagued with cold and fevers — in Mississippi, in late May — and with sore throats. They had enlarged glands throughout the body, secondary to the several infections they chronically suffer. Some of them showed jaundice in their eyes, which meant that liver damage was likely, or that hemolysis secondary to bacterial invasion had occurred.

What particularly saddened and appalled us were the developmental anomalies and diseases that we know once were easily correctable, but now are hopelessly consolidated. Bones, eyes, vital organs that should long ago have been evaluated

and treated are now all beyond medical assistance, even if it were suddenly — incredibly *is the word the people themselves* feel *rather than use* — available. In some cases we saw children clearly stunted, smaller than their age would indicate, drowsy and irritable.

In sum, children living under unsanitary conditions without proper food, and with a limited intake of improper food, without access to doctors or dentists, under crowded conditions in flimsy shacks pay the price in a plethora of symptoms, diseases, aches, and pain. No wonder that in Mississippi (whose Negroes comprise 42 percent of the state's population) the infant mortality rate among Negroes is over twice that of whites; and while the white infant mortality rate is dropping, the rate for Negroes is rising.

Perhaps more valuable and instructive were the comments of five Mississippi doctors who were asked by the state's governor, Paul B. Johnson, to visit the same counties we visited — "in response to certain charges of starvation and conspiracy in the state of Mississippi." Many people in the state, not only doctors and politicians, felt that once again "outsiders" had come upon the Delta and the South to tarnish and malign its "traditions," to single out unfairly this area, that region — when all over the country certain people have trouble finding work, a decent place to live, and even enough food to appease their hunger, their children's hunger. Let our own doctors go see what *really* exists, Mississippi's governor said — and by prompting such a step he provided the kind of leadership the nation certainly craves and doesn't always find. Here are some observations from the medical report submitted to Governor Johnson, and then to the United States Senate:

The situations encountered were indeed primitive. In one locality eight families were found to share one faucet and one privy. The mother of one of these families stated that she obtained surplus commodity food and that her welfare check was seventy-one dollars per month. She said she had been unable to get work for some time. Her monthly rent is fifteen dollars. She has no children in either of the Head Start programs, but her house does have electricity and a new refrigerator. Sanitation in the area was not acceptable by modern standards. Six of her eight children were seen. Several of them had infected lesions and all appeared to have some degree of anemia, but none was on the verge of starvation.

At one house visited, there was one outdoor privy serving "nine or ten families." Not far away was a single water faucet which constituted the only water supply for the same people. Garbage and refuse were strewn about the premises and the smell of human excrement was unmistakable. . . .

Hospital facilities for indigent patients are virtually nonexistent. . . .

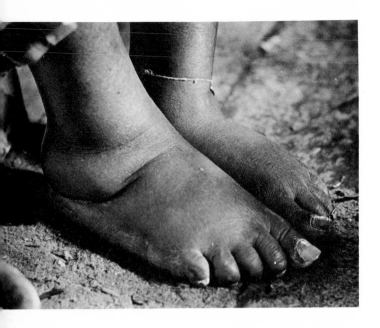

Starvation in the sense that children or persons are actually dying from the lack of food in Washington or Bolivar Counties does not exist. . . . There are, however, children and adults who are living in extreme poverty situations which are detrimental to health. Some have very inadequate housing, very inadequate clothes, very inadequate medical and dental care and a diet that is inadequate in terms of quality and balance. This is due in part to the following: a) Low income: Welfare checks are not adequate. The average adult receives forty-five dollars per month and the average child only twelve dollars. The average Aid to Dependent Children family grant is only thirty-eight dollars per family per month. The state is now paying only 28 percent of its legally authorized grant. b) Ignorance of the parents: There is a basic lack of education in budgeting monies, meal planning, food preparation, the proper types of food for a baby, and fundamental personal hygiene. c) Overloaded health and welfare staff: These staffs have the highest case loads in the United States, and are able to provide only "touch and go" attention to some of these people's problems. The state agencies we consulted, primarily the Public Health Department and the Public Welfare Department, are doing an extremely good job with the facilities and the monies available to them. We believe that they know the answers to their problems and have the know-how to go about solving them, if they had more money with which to train and employ personnel and expand their facilities. . . .

In summary, the situation as observed in Humphreys County does not appear to be markedly different from that in Leflore County. Here, also, there are persons who are underhoused, underfed, undereducated and underemployed. Some of them lack sufficient medical care and hospital facilities and many are virtually unemployable. Through the two Head Start programs an effort is being made to improve the lot of children in the four- and five-year age groups, but here again, there is overlapping of activity, reduplication of facilities, and competition for financial support. . . .

There it is — from distinguished physicians who live and practice medicine in the state of Mississippi. They come from a profession that is generally regarded as particularly conservative, and from a state that votes regularly to support what are called conservative policies. It would be hard to see how those doctors or the governor who appointed them and later submitted their report to the Congress of the United States of America can be considered "wild-eyed" radicals or worse.

In point of fact it was what they could not *escape* seeing that prompted the essentially "radical" document they authored. They became sober-eyed and distressed. Like the rest of us, they had managed for a long time to avoid or shun what anyway was not in the cards for them to look at. They are leading medical authorities in their state, yet for a long time they did not meet up with the very sickest people in that state. Who, indeed, has the right to single out them or their state for particular condemnation — when children from all over this land face conditions not at all unlike those described in the report requested by Governor Johnson?

Some of the children those doctors saw can now be seen by all of us in this book. The faces, the landscape, the concrete, physical reality is all here for our eyes to behold and scan and capture and send along those neural pathways to our central nervous systems, to what neurologists call the "hind-brain," where emotions like rage and horror and terrible sadness lie buried or not-so-buried, hidden or merely waiting — for expression, to be spoken and heard and felt by others. Our eyes also dispatch what we see to those precious and singular "frontal lobes," the pride of man. There we sort things out and come to terms with them. There we think.

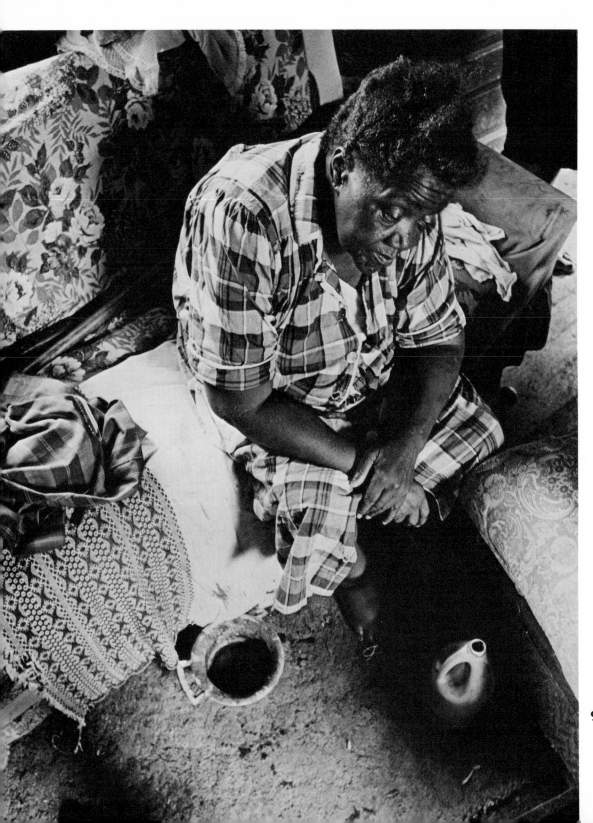

There we beget understanding. There our sensibilities are born, live on, and in moments of real truth, exert themselves mightily. There we receive the brunt of all our built-in wildness and primitivism; and there we turn "emotions" to powerful ideas and to beliefs that command attention and devotion. There pictures and "data" mix — and somehow, sometimes, become refined into, honed into, a thing called "enlightenment" or "judicious concern" or "civilized indignation" or "compassionate, thoughtful protest." There, finally, we discover "balance" and weigh our security, our social security. When we have done so, when we have considered how much of our own skin, our own comfort we are ready to jeopardize for the sake of the next fellow — then we are ready to defend ourselves, to call one man "too upset," another "too sympathetic," another "too outraged," still another "too idealistic" about this or that to realize the practical, complex, complicated, intricate, longstanding, incredibly difficult and resistant nature of — oh, just about any "problem" that is described these days.

So, life is not mere emotion — be it a feeling of hunger or a feeling of moral outrage. In a civilized society, an advanced technological one, "thinking, responsible men," men with power in their hands, must delay things, decide on "priorities," choose the "important ones for now," assign the rest to "later." The same thing goes for the children whom Mr. Clayton bothers us with so repeatedly in this book. They also have to do something with their lives, with the choices they have or don't have, with the "raw" emotions that flood them no less than us. While we consider them one

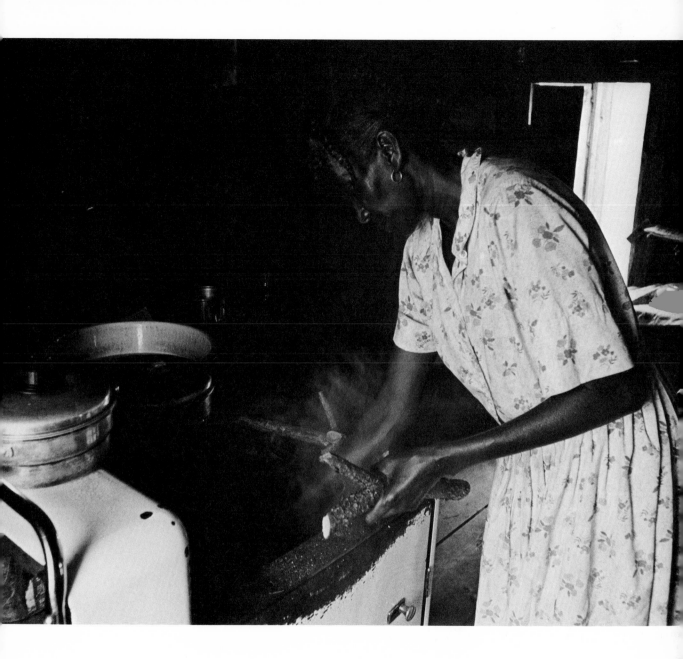

part of the "challenge" to a great world power, they day by day achieve what I suppose can be called a "world view" — of which "we" are assuredly a part. They begin to learn exactly what is permitted and what is impossible, what is encouraged and what is done on pain of death. They also begin to learn what pain is, what it means to get up in the morning and feel the skin itch, or pour out pus, or send messages of hurt and injury back "inside" to the brain. They begin to expect things: this arm doesn't quite work, or that leg. The presence of a dull, aching pain in the stomach is the way it is, the way it has to be. An accident or an injury are followed by nothing much — no trips to a doctor, no stay in a hospital, no medicines, no bandages and splints and advice and special attention. When the weather is cold, it is cold everywhere — in the fields, up the hollows, by the creek, or inside the house. When summer comes, it too cannot be contained — by an air-conditioner, or by screens that keep out flies and mosquitoes, or by fans, or by lots of cold showers or by vacations to the seashore or to the mountains, or by going abroad. And school — yes, there are schools: a one-room shack here; a new building there, full nevertheless of teachers who don't themselves know whether "it's of any use, the little learning we offer these children."

So spoke one of them when I asked her to describe her work:

We try, a lot of us do. I know some of us
don't even care any more. But a lot of
us try. We try to give these children a
few hours of order and discipline. We try
to teach them — and at least every day
they come here we have one meal for
them, and we try to keep the building neat

and orderly for them. You know, they're not used to that, a lot of them aren't. But after a while I think they begin to think we're not real, *we're* the exception. I mean, they'll tell you, even the most silent ones by the time they're here a year or two, they'll tell you. They'll say there's no point to it all, that they just as soon stay home, that you can't do any better with education than without it, not around here. We tell them to close their mouths and stop talking like that, or they'll get into trouble, lots of trouble. Then you know what? They say they know. They say they know that you don't say a word to the white man, because he'll kill you, that's what he'll do around here. But they want us to know what they think, what they've decided. It's hard, very hard — on them and of course on us, the conscientious teachers who stay here and do the best we can. You can say we're no good — that's what some of the civil-rights people say — but someone has to be here, even in the worst places, with the segregationists running the state. Someone has to be here, even if we don't do much good. The kids at least have to know that there is something called a school, and that if a lot of other changes occurred, the school would be better, and would be a place they woudn't mind coming to at all. As it is, though, they do mind. I admit that.

What do they "mind"? What is *on* their minds? After a few years one of the children Mr. Clayton has photographed can indeed get to know an outsider, at least know him well enough to abandon his silence and fear and suspicion and an unspeakable kind of mocking, wondering, smiling, laughing sensibility for a moment of wry speech:

Things as they are around here — well, they're not too good. That's what my momma says to me. They're not too good. She says someday they might get better. She says they would, they'd get better if we went up there to Chicago. She and my daddy, all the time they say no, it's bad there too, or yes, we're going tomorrow, or maybe next week. Then something comes up, and we never seem to leave; we never get there, to Chicago; or anywhere that I can see; just here; and once a month into the town, to get food for to eat for the month; and to church, we go every Sunday there; and that's all. Oh, I forgot school. Some days I'll go, and some days not. The teachers want you all dressed up, and they tell me it's not only that I haven't got the right clothes, it's that I have this bad thing on my head — it's a rash, and it may be something catching, she says, "For all I know it may be catching," that's what she said, yes sir. So if it gets better for a while — yes sir, it does — I'll try me the school. I'll wear my brother's shoes. They're mine, too; but he says they're his because he's the older one. And I'll go. Once I was there all week.

100

*Well, I think I'd like to try being a pilot
on one of those airplanes. They fly over
here, going to the Air Force base.
Sometimes they fly so low I figure I could
touch them if I was up there on top of
the tree. I figure they can see me down
here, they can, when they fly so low — so
I shout up at them. I say "hello," and I
say, "You're a real big plane," and once I
said, "Hey, stop over there; you can land
on the field, near the cotton and we could
come look in." But he was gone before I
finished telling him.*

It won't be long, of course, until that
twelve-year-old child is much, much "older."
At twelve, like most of his friends, he is vir-
tally through with school. Many of them
are going steady, and in a year or two will
be thinking of marriage. What is more, at
home and in the neighborhood he is no longer
looked upon as a child. He is growing, even
grown. He knows his way around. He knows
how to speak to bosses and sheriffs and store-
keepers. He has weathered a full decade of life
and more. He is a *survivor*. Though one such
boy tends to be shy and laconic, let me connect
together remarks he has made to me over the
years:

*I guess you see a lot here, as much as any
place. Now that I'm out of school I get to
see even more. School wasn't much of
anything but a waste. The teachers didn't
do much. They just shouted at you and
made you feel real bad. Whatever you
did, they were on you, telling you it
wasn't good, and it wouldn't lead you any*

101

place. They'd be asking us every morning
if we wanted to be like our momma and
our daddy, and if that was the case we
could go ahead, but we'd pay for it later.
And they said if we minded them — well,
then we'd go way up, to I don't know
where. And when I told them I didn't
believe them, I didn't believe we'd go
any place but where we were, be
we in school or not — well, that
was when she told me, the teacher told
me that the time was drawing near for me
to leave and go sit at home with my
daddy. I was about to stop anyway. You
get to be over ten and it's no good,
sitting there, hearing them. You're too
big for the chair and they don't know

what to do with you anyway. They just
want the little kids, to lead about for a
little while, until they won't oblige any
longer.

I don't know about later. I feel pretty
good now — not all better, but OK. I
haven't had a fit for a while, and they tell me
my blood is stronger from the new blood
they gave me a while back. I help around
the house all the time. We watch each
other, and we figure things to do, the
others and me. I go for the water
sometimes, and I see my friends a lot. If
there's any spare work in town, they know
they can come get us. They send out a
truck and we goes to help them — if

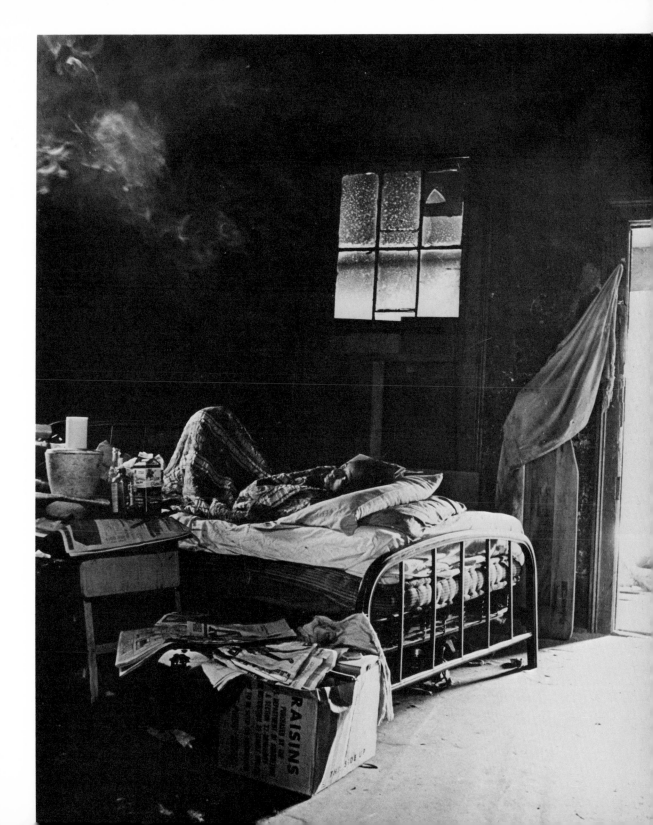

*there is cleaning to do, or the lawns to
care for, or things like that. You can clear
yourself a few dollars every few weeks
if you're real lucky, though there's more
of us than there is work, I believe that.
The best thing you can do, though, is get
yourself a good woman to marry. If she
knows someone in town who will give her
a regular job — housework, like that —
then you're really set up. You don't have
to worry about groceries. You can always
buy them if you have a little money
coming in each week.*

The women he is talking about make ten or
fifteen dollars a week, and no doubt about it,
that helps at the food store. He has his eye on
a girl, a year older, that he wants to marry soon.
They don't know where they'll live or how, but
that is a worry for tomorrow. I am quite sure
they know one another intimately well. They
watch television all the time, in fact know more
about what is going on in the world than
friendly and in various ways condescending
observers like me are apt to let themselves discover. One day I had the nerve to ask them —
I tried to do it in a casual way — who the governor was and what they thought about him.
The young woman of thirteen replied quickly:

*Johnson. He's gone back on himself. He
used to sound real bad. You might have
thought he would be the worst one we've
ever had. But he's been quiet-sounding
since he's been governor. He doesn't say
much that's too bad. And if he hasn't
brought much help to us — well, my
daddy says no governor here can. We
just have to accept that, and try to do*

*what we can for ourselves. That's what
he says. Me, I tend to think we should go
ask for more. That's the direction it seems
to be, more and more. Our minister said
so a few weeks ago. He said it didn't
mean we were going to Heaven because
we are poor. So, we might as well try to
get something more if we can — as well
as pray. Now that's how I see it.*

Soon they will be married, and I don't know
whether they'll stay or move on to Birmingham
or New Orleans or up north. I do know that she
is nearly as anemic as he has been, and I do
know that an anemic woman suffers a much
higher incidence of spontaneous abortions and
miscarriages, gives birth to more retarded children, and in general is weak and tired before an
inevitably yelling, crying, and hungry child ap-
pears before her to herald a new set of possibilities — and probabilities of disaster.

Again and again we can only say: so it goes,
"world without end." From time to time I look
at the photographs that Walker Evans or Dorothea Lange took in the thirties and seem to recognize the same white and Negro families I work
with today. And yet, things have changed very
much — not only for "us," to whom the "great
depression" is a distant, bitter memory, or
merely a piece of history one now studies in
class, but for "them," too. Why should the very
poorest be exempted from the cliché that ap-
pearances do not tell all? I do not believe the
people Mr. Clayton has enabled us to see are
quite the ones Agee and Evans met in Alabama,
or Dorothea Lange saw in her travels through
America in the thirties. The American setting has
changed: the cars, the roads, the styles of cloth-
ing, the general environment that even the very
poor share with everyone else. Somehow the

work here. The business people and the government, they send their money and their new factories to other places.

He is not poor by any means. He is a doctor. He is well-read; yet, as he says, in the most remote of hollows his patients — and the many he cannot and does not see — know what he knows: "They know more about what's going on than they used to know — and it's harder on them than it used to be when there weren't many of us that well off."

We realize all that, I suppose — when we stop to think about it. Walker Evans and Dorothea Lange moved thousands of Americans to shame and indignation and sympathy and a sense of longing — to say something, to do something that would *change* things, so that the toughness, the persistence, the desperate strength in people barely able to stay fed, clothed, and under a roof would not prove wasted. Yes, Mr. Clayton may help us become more determined, more curious about America — all of it. Certainly he has not held back. In picture after picture he spares himself and us very little. Like a physician he bears down on details, on lesions and swellings and lumps and deformities. He catches machines doing their work and havoc, or water standing about in gutters and amid debris. He does not seem predominantly interested in "composition," in an artistic presentation — and yet his pictures grow and grow as one by one they speak to us about birth, growth, decay, death — and always the struggle that American citizens must make between sunrise and sunset and sunset and sunrise. The children cry and play and seek one another out and rest out of fatigue and hunger and boredom. Their parents care — their faces will smile or frown or look impassive and suspicious and amused and expectant and utterly

people in this book seem different — perhaps more lonely, more confused by the ironies and paradoxes that this nation presents to them as much as to those of us who feel educated and sensitive. In West Virginia last year I heard this from an elderly man:

> *A while back you knew you had a lot of company. You'd tune in on the radio and hear Mr. Roosevelt telling the whole country that we were in a hell of a state and we all had to pull together. Then the war came, the Second World War, and then the Korean one, and a lot of people got it better, but things stayed still here, dead still. In fact they got worse. It makes you ashamed. You wonder what you did, or what you didn't do. You can't say it's laziness, either. We just don't have*

jaded. Their grandparents look doomed and defiant and resigned and tired beyond all exhaustion and still they are capable of being puzzled and stimulated — still able to seek the decent living conditions that in themselves enable any man or woman to be no better or worse than his neighbor, but at least strong enough to find a destiny other than constant pain, hunger, uncertainty, and terror.

In any event, all that is shown here has been brought to "us," brought to our cities by people who have had to move or else die. These are the people who reluctantly or eagerly have come to "the big places," to "the avenues where there are the big buildings." They leave the inheritance Mr. Clayton has so painstakingly documented for streets that border on our own; and the last pictures in this book show where they go. They have become our neighbors, our urban neighbors, close at hand, around the corner, at our very threshold — far more so than perhaps we frankly care to acknowledge. One way or another, "they" have become "us." One way or another, we will have to make one another's acquaintance — because the odds are overwhelming that our slums or ghettos will increase and increase over the next few years:

I see the planes fly over here, and I want to go where they go, up North a lot of them. But I don't know if I should try it. I'd stay here if I thought it would get any better, or I'd go there if I thought it was worth it. But when I'm in a real low mood, you know what I think? I think it don't really make that much difference, either way. Probably, though, we'll all be in some city or other, the way it's going down here. They're pushing on us all the time to "git, git, git" — that's what the bossman *says, "Git, because we've got no use for you any more." He even told me there are a lot of white people he thought should leave where they are and go someplace else. Now, there's a fair man for you.*

Incredible, utterly incredible that an American, that such a man — bright, shrewd, imaginative, almost illiterate, hungry, ragged, jobless, witty, philosophical, tired, disappointed, proud, searching, downcast, and sore — has to live the kind of life he is now living. In his presence — out of my shame and fear and nervousness and yes, arrogance, namely a desire to convince him and myself that he may be powerless but someone like me can summon words, can muster effective outrage — I have offered my "help," spoken my wish that the billions and billions of dollars that *our* country possesses would one day be spent differently, so that not a single citizen of this country would go hungry. "Maybe so.

109

Maybe so. I don't think I'll live to see that day," was his reply. He saw me seeing his "despair," his "hopelessness." (I suppose that's all I can do, turn his lifetime of *experience,* of expectations and disappointments, into a few static words, like "despair" or "hopelessness," or even worse, "depression.") Then, he suddenly did something else — by saying something else: "Don't worry, though. I tell my kids we'll somehow make it. I'll get by until tomorrow, and they'll get by longer, I hope. And some one of us, he'll be the lucky one to have it good, like you say."

Exactly who needs "help" and "reassurance" in this nation — that man or those who feel sorry for him but can't do a thing to change their sorrow into deeds? Perhaps one day we will all be better citizens — when that man has a better life and our lives are on the way to becoming better because of that fact alone. Meanwhile, in anticipation of Mr. Clayton's sad, awful, lovely, tender, brutal photographs I can only make a few concluding, summarizing observations, rather in the fashion (one vaguely recalls) of the sentences on pages of books children use in elementary school — because everything Mr. Clayton's camera presents to us is so terribly simple, so direct, so obvious, so *there,* waiting for action.

When a doctor sees a child who is sick he may well be seeing the last stage in what I suppose we ought to call a bit formidably a *process.* That is, a disease may be the final confrontation between a littered, chaotic, deteriorated, contaminated, unsanitary, and in fact poisonous "outside" world and the child's body, his "inner" world of growing but needy and vulnerable blood vessels, muscles, bones, vital organs, and skin.

The trash and waste around a child's home are not inert; they harbor germs, flies, and rats.

Stagnant water also encourages germ-bearing flies and mosquitoes.

The child is lucky if his home has electricity and available water. For that matter, he is lucky if his home is not one day, suddenly and arbitrarily, crushed to rubble by strip-miners and their machines. Anyway, electricity can only go so far in easing a burden in a rural shack, and water can be "available" and "running" but not safe or in any way convenient.

The child is lucky if he can take a bathroom for granted — its water, its protection from extreme cold.

A child has to take what he gets — and as a result live or die. He learns about God, and he learns about Man, and what Man has come to call the "environment." He slowly begins to learn which home is *his* . . . and which homes belong to others.

And he learns about food — whether it comes from a supermarket, or a nearby farm, or in the form of commodities, emergency supplies from the government.

At birth the child is already a "medical statistic," among other things. He is delivered in a hospital by a doctor and pronounced healthy, or he is delivered at home and afflicted with defects — an umbilical hernia, or a persistent gastrointestinal complaint.

As he grows, the child becomes alert and responsive, or he learns to be fearful and suspicious, to sleep a lot, even when picked up and held, and when awake to be fretful and unsmiling. He or she may have a scalp infection or a skin disease or a harelip — all of which seem like the usual "out-of-order" things around.

Children, of course, cling to their parents. A mother and father *are* the child's world. The child may be hungry or in pain; with his mother or his grandmother or his father, he has at least all the protection he has come to find possible.

Parents feed children, sometimes regularly and well, sometimes unpredictably, with a piece of bread, a Coke, or better, milk, an apple, and meat.

Parents can't always feed their children well, though; and the children's appearance and "health" testify to that fact; and the sad look on a parent's face also testifies to that fact. It does not take a doctor to see a child who needs medical and surgical help. It does not take a psychiatrist to see how bitter a mother becomes when she cannot offer food to a hungry, crying child. The doctor can direct his attention to the child's skin, his belly, his scarred or twisted limbs, his dazed or confused look. The "ordinary" observer can see the same grim truth for himself — and does not require medical terminology for "confirmation."

No matter how poor and hungry, children cling tenaciously to whatever life, whatever "community" they have found as a birthright. They huddle together, or they go off by themselves — figuratively, with a look, or literally.

Eventually, they grow up — and whatever they have suffered and lacked and missed becomes all too relentlessly obvious. One can see their skin. One can see swollen glands or nodules or a goiter. One can see retardation that has never been challenged or given its own dignity. One can see the feet, or one can see the teeth.

And in those who *do* survive, who live out a reasonably long if hard and uncertain life, one can see those final moments — of awful, stoic endurance, such as William Faulkner described and tried to comprehend.

It is also possible to find old men who are puzzled, but stubbornly determined to keep trying, and old women who do their best each day, with meal after meal, with chore after chore.

There are sick and tired ones, too. It is, perhaps, better not to get very close to them. Their faces, their eyes, tell a thousand dreary, sad "everyday" stories.

Eventually, for many, there is the *decisive* story — of the "move," of the moment when one city beckons people who hate to leave or cannot wait to go. And indeed they *have* gone, gone to the cities; they have gone and gone and gone, by the millions in this century. Black and white, they have gone, and now that they are there, they are "here," with us. We face them. They confront us. Their violent, violated past becomes a fearful presence to us. Their history makes history right before our eyes; and we find out not only who they are and what they are like, and what they have become, but what we have done. We learn about our own history. Perhaps, but only perhaps, we will learn to make for all of us a new history. Particularly to young Americans — who are studying history, who are learning and want to learn — the urge rises to cry out with questions: Will the tired old, stale old excuses and evasions forever keep us paralyzed? Or will the might and wealth of this country once and for all be summoned to the side of the people we see in this book, so they can at last eat decently and work honorably — and so the rest of us in the cities can have at least one less important reason not to lie nervously, fearfully awake?

115

ABOUT THE AUTHOR

Robert Coles, a staff psychiatrist with the Harvard University Health Services, works with black and white people in the rural south, in Appalachia, and in urban ghettos. He is a consultant to the Southern Regional Council and to the Appalachian Volunteers as well as a member of the National Advisory Committee on Farm Labor. Dr. Coles is the author of *Children of Crisis: A Study of Courage and Fear,* and is currently working on a sequel to that book.

ABOUT THE PHOTOGRAPHER

Al Clayton was born in 1934 in a small copper-mining town in Southeast Tennessee. At eighteen he left to join the Navy, where he remained for six years. During that time he became interested in photography and continued his studies at the Art Center School in Los Angeles. His photographs have appeared in such publications as *Look, Atlantic Monthly, Time,* and *Newsweek. Still Hungry in America* is his first book.

Some who have worked their way through these words and these pictures—in surprise,
in sadness, in shame and anger—may want to *do* something.
The Southern Regional Council, a nationally respected nonprofit organization,
has agreed to receive contributions from private citizens—all of which
will go to a recently established Committee to Aid Hungry Americans.
Members of the Committee have been drawn from those
who work alongside poor and hungry people in the various sections of the nation.
All gifts will quickly become translated into food
that will go directly to those who need it.

Robert Coles

The address of the Southern Regional Council is:

5 Forsyth Street
Atlanta, Georgia 30303

The publisher has agreed to donate a portion of its profits to the Committee to Aid Hungry Americans.